PROJECTS ARE PEOPLE, TOO!

A guide to getting along so you can GET SOME WORK DONE

FAITH KNIGHT PMP, MSPM

Projects Are People, Too
A guide to getting along so you can get some work done

Published by:
   Copy: FRESH, LLC
   P.O. Box 895
   Lithonia, GA 30058

All Rights Reserved. No part of this book may be reproduced or transmitted in any form or by any means, electronic or mechanical, including photocopying, recording or by an information storage and retrieval system without written permission from the author, except for the inclusion of brief quotations in a review.

Edited by Kacy Cook
Illustration by Dave Kirwan
Design and Layout by John Andrews Design

Copyright © 2011 Faith Knight

ISBN-13: 978-0-9826190-2-5
Printed in the USA

*To Uncle Bill,
a true project manager*

Table of Contents

Acknowledgments	7
Introduction	9
Personality Types & The Project Team	15
Getting Off To A Good Start	27
You, Them, Us	37
Attitudes And Agendas	49
Office Politics	65
The 5 Ws And H	77
Indirect Messaging	93
Managing To Motivate	107
Putting It All Into Perspective	125
Bibliography	131
Table Of Figures	134
About The Author	135

Acknowledgments

I would like to thank my husband for the continued support he provides; my editor, Kacy Cook, whose expertise came at the right time; my family who is always there to read what's coming next; John Andrews who fit me into his busy schedule to make sure this book looked great both inside and out.

Thank you.

Introduction

Remember when you were a kid, and you would observe adult behavior — watching not just how your parents acted but other relatives, too?

As you absorbed your surroundings, you began to wonder what made them act in certain ways. For instance, why did Uncle Joe always rush down to the basement with Dad when he and Aunt Emily arrived for dinner? He always seemed to be in a big hurry to get away from her. You wondered why he never showed the kind of affection for his wife that your mom and dad had for each other. There were no warm conversations, not even a peck on the cheek every now and then.

Then, as you got older, you began to realize it probably had something to do with the way Aunt Emily sprang into a tirade of complaints the moment she hit the front porch.

She'd say to your mother, "Why don't you ever sweep out here, Abigail?" And once inside, it was everything from "How can you let Ralph lounge around this house on the weekends when there's work to be done?" to "Little Timothy is a bit old to still be sucking his thumb, isn't he?"

It was an endless barrage of dissatisfaction in a myriad of things over which she had no control and, worse, absolutely no business.

As a child you often wondered why Uncle Joe kept quiet about it. And being a kid with no sense of protocol, you might have asked him that very question. That's when he'd wrap his arm around your waist, pinch your nose and say, "Don't mind your aunt; that's just the way she is."

But once you entered adulthood, you surmised that, at some time during the course of their 35-year marriage, Uncle Joe must have agonized over her behavior before he just gave up trying to change it. That was his way of managing Aunt Emily's personality: It was something he had to live with. It came with the package.

Your friends and acquaintances come with likes, dislikes and quirks, too. Even you have some of your own. These things are what make us human. They define us. And for better or worse, they are ingrained in us to the point that we hardly notice their existence. That is, until someone points them out. Then we are either shocked and in disbelief or we acknowledge the behavior as a weakness we just can't seem to get a handle on. It doesn't mean we are bad people. It doesn't mean we necessarily have to change. What it does mean is that others have to put up with us…at home and at work.

The variety of personalities you will encounter on your professional projects will likely make you want to react differently than Uncle Joe did. You may want to shut irritating characters out of the process or discount their contributions. But you can't. Projects must continue. And if you do take the path of least resistance — simply ignoring certain co-workers — it will likely cause more problems than it solves.

One of the first things you learn in any project management course is that the only constant on a project is change. In contrast, the personalities you encounter on your team likely will not change. Just like Aunt Emily, members will have moods, unexpected motivations and pessimistic outlooks. It's the unavoidable result of working side by side with your fellow human beings.

The focus of this book is to make you aware of challenges you will face from personalities on team projects, including typical motivations, and how to commence relationship building so the project doesn't become derailed.

We'll examine the five major areas of personality, known as the "Big Five" or "five-factor model," based on research by D.W. Fiske and others. We'll review popular personality tests and how they can assist in understanding project members' motivations.

You'll read about real-world personality clashes you may face and discover how to keep your projects on track despite the disruptions.

You'll get advice on how to approach a new project and team members. You'll also learn how to analyze and manage a variety of situations.

It's no secret that a project is shaped in part by the organization that creates it as well as by the organization's related culture. We will see how company culture can affect your ability to manage your team and what effect it can have on the success or failure of a project.

We'll address ways to leverage certain personality traits

to move your agenda forward, and look at how particular PM leadership styles can assist you. We'll also take a look ahead to see what challenges are on the horizon for project teams as the Baby Boomer generation retires.

All of this is an effort to equip you with tools to ensure that personality-related issues don't overrun your projects.

I hope you will use the experience and wisdom here to guide you throughout your project management career.

Personality Types & The Project Team

Real World Advice:
"Understand the strong points of each member
and give them the work they enjoy."
— R.C., Computer Business Services

The one thing most project managers dread when starting a new project is working with people. It's true. For instance, if you are an engineer, you may prefer to manage the actual tasks of a project rather than the varied personnel who carry them out. But like it or not, as a PM, you must acquire the arts of negotiation, communication, conflict management and, my favorite, restraint.

Let's jump right in by assessing where you fall on the "people pleaser" spectrum. Just answer the following seven questions:

A. When I'm on a business flight I most enjoy sitting beside...
   - ◯ 1) chatty, large people wearing lots of cologne.
   - ◯ 2) crying children.
   - ◯ 3) children.
   - ◯ 4) an empty seat.
   - ◯ 5) two empty seats.

B. During a company meeting I most enjoy...
   - ◯ 1) watching a long, dry PowerPoint presentation.
   - ◯ 2) people repeating themselves. Again.
   - ◯ 3) people texting constantly.
   - ◯ 4) frequent breaks.
   - ◯ 5) leaving.

C. I love it when my coworker...
   - ◯ 1) watches YouTube videos on his PC.
   - ◯ 2) eats stinky food at his desk.
   - ◯ 3) clips his nails.
   - ◯ 4) calls in sick.
   - ◯ 5) quits.

D. I like my boss most when he...
   - ◯ 1) e-mails me every half-hour.
   - ◯ 2) peers over my shoulder.
   - ◯ 3) jokes about firing me.
   - ◯ 4) is delayed flying home.
   - ◯ 5) is on vacation.

E. My least favorite office noise is somebody...
- ○ 1) clearing his throat.
- ○ 2) slurping his coffee.
- ○ 3) tapping his pencil.
- ○ 4) squeaking his desk chair.
- ○ 5) snapping his gum.

F. I love overhearing workplace conversations about...
- ○ 1) the boyfriend.
- ○ 2) the girlfriend.
- ○ 3) the spouse.
- ○ 4) the kids.
- ○ 5) how much someone hates his job.

G. The office food I like least is...
- ○ 1) vending-machine sandwiches.
- ○ 2) onion bagels.
- ○ 3) cardboard pizza.
- ○ 4) Tupperware Surprise.
- ○ 5) hand-fouled candy from an open dish.

So how do you think you did? Add up your scores then check them against the scores below:

1-7 You really do like people. Consider seeking professional help.
8-13 There's hope: you're not a total glutton for punishment.
14-21 Clearly, you're on the path to realizing that people

aren't all they're cracked up to be.
22-29 You are a People Hater. Although you have natural talent, you could use some additional skills.
30-35 You are a devout People Hater. Welcome, friend! Get ready to turn your natural skills into business assets.

To be honest, asking you to take this quiz — from the book *I Hate People* (Littman & Hershon, 2009) — was a tongue-in-cheek attempt to get you to think about the extent of your people skills.

Foremost in your quest to manage personalities on a project is determining how you feel about certain kinds of people. Let's begin with a review of the most common personality types and their characteristics.

Researchers have conducted numerous studies on personality traits and, over the years, they've determined that every personality falls under at least one of the following descriptors:
• Extraversion — outgoing, social, assertive
• Agreeableness — friendly, trusting, cooperative
• Conscientiousness — committed, concerned, dependable
• Neuroticism — self-conscious, anxious, pessimistic
• Openness — artistic, curious, imaginative

Not all psychologists agree on the definitions of these descriptors; however, most do agree that the model is a valid starting point for analyzing complex and varied human behaviors.

In the *Journal of Organizational Behavior* (Thoms,

Moore, & Scott, 1996), the study's authors quote several source works that define each of these personality factors. The focus of their study, however, was to determine which traits would work best in self-directed teams (the dynamics of which we will discuss in subsequent chapters) but are equally applicable to other types of groups, such as the conventional project team.

Noteworthy in their study is that, of the five factors, neither *openness* nor *agreeableness* correlated well to self-directed teams. Thoms et al. did not suggest any rhyme or reason for their findings, but simply noted that the results were not what they expected.

Those results did not surprise me, however.

I'm not a psychologist, but it is my experience that people working on teams who portray themselves as agreeable tend to be that way to maintain order in the world around them. That does not mean they are necessarily in favor of the direction things are headed; rather, it's a resignation of sorts. Often, their agreeable nature is meant to appease the team. The trouble develops when they communicate to those outside the team. For example, after leaving a decision-making project session, the "agreeable" person may get with outsiders and paint a negative picture of what took place, while removing himself from responsibility. He just "went along" with the program, he tells them. This behavior tends to sow seeds of discontent and gives an impression of exclusion that is meant to undermine the project. This may have been his intent all along: not to truly agree, but only to leave that impression.

Those dubbed as "open" may find the project boring and

prefer to get on to more interesting pursuits. Their behavior in a decision-making meeting may simply be acts of tolerance rather than genuine objectivity. Back in "the day" we used to hear the term "I'm open" a lot. It meant that the person was fine with whatever was decided, having no real desire to go in one direction or another. That kind of openness can derail a project if you have too many team members who aren't invested in the outcome.

A project team depends on each member's constructive input, even if it is in conflict with the ideas of other team members. While on the surface they appear commendable, the personality factors of agreeableness and openness can betray a lack of genuine interest and team commitment.

So what personality type works well on a project team? Of the three remaining factors — extroversion, conscientiousness and neuroticism — the latter is definitely out. Although I would stake my life on the fact that there is a little neurosis in all of us, the unconstructive behaviors associated with this factor renders it last on the list of desirable traits. On the other hand, team members who are committed (conscientiousness) and outgoing (extroversion) can assist the PM in getting a project off to a good start and continuing on a positive and productive path. Unfortunately, that magical mix rarely happens, so understanding some of the personalities on your team will at least help you to manage them.

There are a number of ways to discover these.

One way is for you and your team to prepare for each other's quirks by taking one of several available personality tests. One of these is the Myers-Briggs Type Indicator®(MBTI®). A mother-daughter team developed this assessment using C. G. Jung's theory of psychological types, which states that people have preferences in the way they take in and organize information.

MBTI uses preferences from these traits: Extroversion or Introversion, Sensing or Intuition, Thinking or Feeling, Judging or Perceiving.

Once determined, these eight preferences yield 16 personality types. People who have taken the MBTI swear by it and can explain to you why they are ESTJ (Extroversion, Sensing, Thinking, Judging) rather than EITJ (Extroversion, Intuition, Thinking, Judging).

If it sounds complex, it is. Still, this instrument has been around since the 1940s, and many firms use it to make determinations about employee personality traits and to make assumptions as to how those traits will translate into the workplace. Like me, you may have already taken the MBTI as part of your project management curriculum.

Another well-received assessment is an empirical approach formally known as the Birkman Method©. According to the official website, this test "accurately measures productive behaviors, stress behaviors, underlying needs, motivations and organizational orientation" (Birkman).

I took the Birkman and found it to be a spot-on indicator of my personal motivators and how I approach projects.

Here are the areas of focus for the 250-question test:

1. **Usual Behavior** — an individual's effective behavioral style (or way of) dealing with relationships and tasks.

2. **Underlying Needs** — an individual's expectations of how relationships and social situations should be governed in context of the relationship or situation.

3. **Stress Behaviors** — an individual's ineffective style of dealing with relationships or tasks; behavior observed when underlying needs are not met.

4. **Interests** — an individual's expressed preference for job titles based on the assumption of equal economic rewards.

5. **Organizational Focus** — the perspective in which an individual views problems and solutions relating to organizational goals.

The test takes a few hours, but when you're finished you will have a readout of your personality based on four predefined "foundation colors": green, red, blue and yellow. For me, this was the most interesting part of the assessment because I was a bit skeptical at first. But once I found out my "color" and its definition, I was a big fan.

I won't get into the specifics of the test, but in a nutshell, here's what the colors mean:

Green — Communicating. These are your salespeople. If the test readout shows a long green bar graph, you are the kind of person who will sell ideas to others. You have the gift of sounding reasonable even if your message turns out to be a crock o' you-know-what. Greens are "the path of least resistance" kind of people. They don't like to make others mad, especially if it is in their best interest to keep them happy.

Blue — Planning. Blue people are very good at laying out a direction for something. They make it look good, too. (Blue people love PowerPoint.) They are strategic and innovative. You obviously need this kind of person on the team during the planning stage of your project.

Yellow — Administrating. Yellows can sit in their office and contemplate until the cows come home. They are analytical by nature and need to understand every little detail before they can agree to lift a finger as it relates to your project. They remind me of the phrase a detective used in the 1960s TV show, *Dragnet*: "Just the facts, ma'am." Yellows are essential during the initiation stage of your project.

Red — Expediting. Reds just want to get it done. They don't want to hear any lip about it; they just want to get from A to Z as soon as possible. As long as you have a Blue working closely with this type, the execution phase is the best place for a Red.

After I took the Birkman test, it was like a light bulb went off in my head. I could finally embrace my "let's just do it" behavior. I was validated. Your team members will be, too. It will help everyone to understand why each behaves in a particular way. Knowledge is comforting. More important, it can assist you in determining which tasks to give to which personality type. Actually, having a project team that possesses a good balance of all the colors will be much more effective.

By the way, if you take this assessment as a group, don't be surprised if the terminology becomes part of the vernacular around the office, with people asking each other "what color are you?"

It's true that tests such as MBTI and Birkman will not solve all of your personality problems. Individuals are complex, and their personalities can vary based on a number of factors, such as environment, social stimuli, and internal or external conflicts.

For instance, how many times on the evening news, have you heard the neighbor of a serial killer say, "He was so nice, and he kept to himself"? Sure, he was nice; that was one aspect of his personality. He obviously had another side.

We tend to act one way among our friends, but we may show a totally different personality around those we dislike. So although the neighbor of the serial killer saw him as a nice guy, she had no knowledge of the man's "totality of behavioral and emotional characteristics," as personality is defined by Webster's dictionary.

When working with people assigned to your project, you, too, will see just one side of the story. However, the longer you work with a person, the more characteristics will come to the fore. Trouble is, as a PM — especially if you are a consultant — you will have little time to assess the subtle nuances of your team members. But you can do the next best thing: you can ask somebody. Some of the most valuable resources a PM consultant has when working in a new company are other PM consultants. Next, we examine how doing a little investigating can go a long way in heading off personality conflicts.

Action Items

✔ **Learn the personality types** of your team members, sponsors and maybe even the client, if you can.

✔ **Try using the MBTI or Birkman** as an exercise in which the whole team can participate. Share the results and discuss which roles would work best on each task.

✔ **Be aware of the five personality types** and what their descriptors can help you glean about your team members' motivations.

✔ Subscribe to the *Journal of Organizational* Behavior. (It can't hurt!)

Getting Off to a Good Start

Real World Advice:
"Be open to learn from people. Listen more."
— O.B., International Development

One of the biggest mistakes I've seen project managers make is what I call the "railroad effect." To understand this concept, visualize a bank takeover. When a bank is declared insolvent, the Federal Deposit Insurance Corp. comes in and literally takes over the daily operations of the bank. With precision and speed, the FDIC employees move in, counting the money, briefing the employees on new procedures, notifying customers and ensuring that the bank continues to provide all expected services without so much as a hint of disruption. If you've never seen one of these takeovers in action, it's awe-inspiring.

But imagine the customers coming into a bank that has been taken over. They are fearful and concerned about the future of their hard-earned money. They have millions of questions, which lead to high anxiety because the atmosphere they were accustomed to has suddenly been turned on its head. It is up to the FDIC crew to put them at ease.

The same kind of trepidation is common for team members when a new PM begins to exhibit the "railroad effect." Their demeanor can become understandably apprehensive and guarded. They don't want you "taking over" their enterprise with new rules or methodologies. They may not even know you, and here you are, swooping in like an eagle to pluck them out of their comfort zone and whisk them off to an unknown place.

It is better to take baby steps and get to know the atmosphere before making any rigid adjustments. Although some projects require a PM to apply the railroad effect — sometimes a PM is brought in to effect sweeping change — there is always time to assess the situation first. If you do, you will gain a greater advantage and improve cooperation. FDIC employees are trained to create an atmosphere of calm. Likewise, it will take silent observation, effective inquiries of the right people and patience on your part to soothe the fears of team members.

I was once hired to sub for a PM representing the client-side on an information technology project (as you know, PMs usually represent the IT side). They needed someone to manage the implementation of a new product, and the IT PM was not serving their needs. During a defect-review meeting, it dawned on me that the team was not tracking defects in any particular manner. The only records they had of who asked for what and when was a bunch of emails. So, turning to the IT PM, I suggested they use a particular tracking tool I knew was already at their disposal. His response was surprising: He didn't need to track the defects!

I was floored. Then I proceeded to tell him in my best inside voice that my superiors needed a way to monitor what IT had been up to over the last three months because the defects had been submitted and no real work had been done.

Despite my best efforts I got nowhere...until I had lunch with a PM consultant who'd been working with this guy for the past year.

"It's not that he doesn't think your idea is good," he told me. "He just doesn't want to be accountable."

He then went on to explain the nuances of the situation, how the guy usually handled conflict, and how to get around it. That lunchtime briefing armed me with the information I needed to manage the situation.

Don't let personalities frustrate you. There is always someone who knows the underlying reasons for certain behaviors. Of course, you may find some people unwilling to share their knowledge — and you might not trust others — but if you feel good about asking, and a person perceives your intent as genuine, you could end up with just the solution you were looking for.

Company Culture

Part of what may lead a team to display resistance is *company culture*. No matter where you work, there is an atmosphere, an *identity* that employees develop and pass on to newcomers who enter their inner circle. Over time, this atmosphere morphs into what's known as the company's culture.

Company culture is not really a bad thing. It helps new employees understand how things are done, what is expected and what is acceptable. It can instill a sense of inclusion and camaraderie and provide stability that allows you to feel part of a common mission.

But herein lies the danger for consultants, contractors and other temporary employees. Ingrained cultures are difficult to overcome and, when you are brought in to lead, the chill created can make you feel like you just stepped into an igloo.

The downside of company culture is that it is often immovable, resistant to change and defensive. You may have noticed this at well-established companies. "Blue chip" and other such corporations that have remained unchanged since the dawn of time are not about to let a stranger come in and start unsettling things. They *like* the way things are; they *built* it that way. Far be it from you to say it should be otherwise!

If you determine that the personality clashes you are experiencing stem from the culture, you will need to tread lightly. You'll need to figure out how to either get around it or live with it.

I was once a PM at a prestigious firm where the culture manifested itself in beige dresses and blue suits. The order of the day was conservative conversation, down-the-nose stares and lots of do's and don'ts. I found myself against that backdrop after spending years at a very laid-back company where the culture was anything but staid.

Despite this difference, I started the first day by trying to run the show, thinking their culture didn't matter. I had a pad and pen in my hand and lots of great, life-changing ideas in my head. I was ready to take on their project, full steam ahead — just lead me to the problem and by-golly I'm gonna fix it!

Little did I realize it, but my approach was making the functional manager very uncomfortable. She never said anything, but every now and then I'd get a furrowed brow and upturned lip, and I knew something was wrong. Being the go-getter that I am, I just kept plugging along, taking over tasks and informing her of my plans in each morning meeting.

One day, she returned from vacation to find that I had changed the process for managing offsite developers. It was a brilliant plan, or at least I thought so, and the developers on both sides said it allowed them to work more closely together. Well, the functional manager taught me a lesson. During a meeting, she took the opportunity to clip my wings! She took over the process and decided to run it herself. I was shocked and didn't understand. Why was she acting that way?

During a lunch conversation with a staffer, I was told that I was not doing things the "company way." I was told that they could not "digest me in one gulp." They needed to ease into a situation; they wanted me to listen and learn first, and then interject my ideas. I'm glad I learned that lesson early in my career. Being too anxious can sometimes rub people the wrong way, and outperforming them is even worse.

From that day on, I handled the functional manager as a co-PM, getting her input on everything before I made a move. Before this revelation, I didn't recognize my place as a newcomer. I was not giving due respect to the experience and prestige the firm and its employees felt they deserved.

The culture at that company valued protocol and recognition of senior leaders. It was similar to a teacher-student relationship, and although I was not crazy about the arrangement, I worked within its boundaries to keep things moving ahead in a positive way.

To some, especially newly graduated PMs, conformance is not a very palatable pill, but it teaches patience and develops wisdom. Recognizing company cultures helps you to accept and respect differences in people, as well as places of employment.

To assist you in managing the varied personalities on a job, follow that tried-and-true strategy: Stop, Look and Listen. *Stop* yourself before you run headlong into a project or a culture. *Look* at what lies before you and try to understand how the culture works. *Listen* to those within the culture to discover what you need to know to be successful. You want to leave a company with a good reputation and a chance to return one day on another project.

Company culture can sometimes be a hindrance, especially for those who are internal project managers. Your intent may be to subvert — or in some way get around — the culture. You may view the project as a catalyst for making some much-needed operational changes.

In this scenario, the culture may be standing between you and progress. Take heed. I've been there. The difference in this situation is that you have to live with the outcome, and that means your strategy in handling the personalities on your team will take a bit more tact. After all, when the project is over you still have to work with those people.

Alternatively, if you're OK with the culture and you just want to get results, going into a project as an internal PM gives you the upper hand. You know what to expect and how things are normally done. You know your limitations, and you may even know your "go to" team members as well as your slackers. Take those gems of knowledge and use them to your advantage.

If you know someone on your team is always late, save the discussion of his or her assignments for last. If someone is typically a "Red," per Birkman, that's the person to handle your risk-related tasks because you know they are sure to get it done.

There may be team members you've seen around the office but don't know well. Ask a trusted co-worker to give you the lowdown on them: how is he or she on projects? Does he toe the company line? Is she a complainer? Is he a straight shooter? Find out all you need to know and then keep that information in your back pocket. You can draw on it when you get to phases of the project where these individuals will either shine or cause chaos. This foreknowledge also gives you the ability to map out a contingency plan, just in case. In this situation knowing and understanding company culture affords you some leverage. For instance, you can reinforce company values by bringing in development trainers to conduct team-building sessions. You can also reiterate the company's mission throughout the project to keep everyone focused on the common goal you all share.

There are many ways to use culture to your advantage as an internal PM. Don't take it for granted; rather, make it work for you.

Action Items

- ✔ On your first day or within the first week at a company find another project manager who has worked there on similar projects and spend time with him or her.

- ✔ **Ask the PM to explain** any do's and don'ts when leading the project team.

- ✔ Find out if there are any personalities on the team who could present challenges and **get advice on how to manage them**.

- ✔ If you cannot find another PM at the company, explain the situation to a colleague outside the company for support and suggestions. **Be confidential!**

- ✔ **Set aside time to get to know your team members** individually before the project shifts into high gear then maintain an open-door policy with them.

- ✔ **Never flex your muscles** when joining an existing project team. Rather, do "as the Romans do" until you can figure out the best approach for implementing your ideas and methods.

- ✔ **Ask the team for their input** and take it into consideration when formulating new processes or improving existing ones.

- ✔ **Bill yourself as the person who has come to help** move the project along, rather than someone who is there to disrupt the status quo.

You, Them, Us

Real World Advice:
"You must remain unemotional,
objective and focused on the solution."
– D.B., IT Consultant

Nothing makes me crazier than cross-departmental strife. In some environments, it's unavoidable. That's because most companies put employees in silos based on job focus, and before you know it, a series of fiefdoms arise. *They* work on one thing; *you* work on another. *They* rarely see you; *you* never think about them.

This divide-and-confuse approach is most apparent at company functions. Did you ever notice how members of certain departments tend to sit together, even on social occasions? It seems silly, but in corporations these divisions are a reality. Knowing that any difference can render you an outsider, how do you effectively manage team members from different worlds?

The first step is to reach out. Don't wait for them to come to you, and especially don't wait until the first team meeting.

If possible, find out who is scheduled to be on the project and give them a call or set up a meeting to introduce yourself. If they are in the same building, go by their offices and just stick your head in. Tell them you are the new PM and that you are looking forward to working with them. That small bit of aisle crossing will go a long way once the project begins to ramp up.

Of course, initiative is not the only ammunition you'll need to quell any perceived tension between departments. Understanding what each group needs from the project is crucial.

Your first thought as PM might be to give most of your attention to the needs of the customer, the sponsor of the project. But other groups may have the leverage and are the key influencers who can make or break a project.

For instance, let's say you are working on a new server installation project sponsored by the technical operations group. It would seem reasonable that they — the sponsor — would be the driving force behind the project. Not true. What actually led to this project was the failure of some existing servers previously purchased by tech ops, so the web support group called them on the carpet for it. Therefore, the new server is not really a tech ops project but is backed and co-sponsored by web support.

You may be asking yourself, "How would I know all that if I am just a contractor?" The answer is you wouldn't know, and you don't need to know. What you do need to know is that you should not take it for granted that your project sponsor is the only entity you must please. Taking sides with or catering to just one group has led many a project manager down the path to unemployment.

The key is to keep in mind that, no matter how many departments you must work with to move the project to completion, each one of them is important and should be considered in all decision-making. Stakeholders can be as varied in their agendas as they are in their expertise. It is always the wise course to discover the depth of their involvement, and then consult them throughout the project, as appropriate.

The following are some typical strife-inducing relationships you are likely to encounter:

Department vs. Department

Cross-departmental discord is typical during project initiation, and this unhappiness usually reveals itself on the faces of those in attendance at the kickoff meeting. I would advise you not to get involved.

I was once on a project where, in the interest of being transparent, the sponsor invited everybody-and-their-mother to the meeting. This was her way of being inclusive of the various departments that would be affected by the new tool that would soon be implemented. The problem was that most of the stakeholders knew they would have little say in the requirements. How? Prior to the meeting they had engaged in side conversations with those close to the project who wanted to share their pain. It turned out that the sponsor's gesture was just a ruse. She was known for not being a team player and had no intention of considering any other group's wishes before her own needs had been met.

Despite this simmering spat, I pressed on and tried my best to keep things on a higher plain; I refused to gossip about the whys and wherefores. I didn't spend my lunch hours joining in on the complaining, even though I had my own issues with the sponsor. By staying above the fray, I was able to remain neutral and gained the trust of all those on the team.

It never pays to take sides or make your personal concerns known to anyone on a project, especially if you are a consultant. Your goal is to get the thing done on time and under budget. That's it. Besides, keeping your nose out of such squabbles will prevent you from getting a reputation as someone who cannot be trusted. After all, the next project at that company may require you to work for the very person you dogged out over lunch!

Internal PMs can also learn from this. Even if you aren't fired for taking sides, you could set yourself up for shunning, meaning no one will want to cooperate with you on the next project. I can't say that they won't work with you, because they may be forced to. But make no mistake -- they won't forget a previous transgression. This is where sabotage comes in. Avoid contributing to it if you can.

Person vs. Person

I am proud to say that I cultivated the quality of being long-suffering after sparring with a colleague who could never see things my way. I was not asking for complete submission; all I wanted was a happy medium. It didn't matter that my approach was based on best practices; she could never bring herself to come on board. She would always respond to my logic with, "No, no, no." It drove me up the wall! She followed this with a "mother may I" speech that included long, drawn-out and half-baked reasons as to why my *proven* approach just wouldn't work. I came so close to asking her to take it outside.

You are going to meet some doozies during your PM career, even some who will make your skin crawl. The sad part is that you are going to have to just let it crawl because the last thing you can afford to do is encourage the start of a battle. Take my advice: being the one to back down has its advantages. Professional disagreements are fine as long as they don't get personal. If you feel like you can't hold your tongue, leave the room. Walk out, but not in a huff. If you can muster up the courtesy, excuse yourself and promise to return shortly. If you are in a team meeting, suggest the topic be tabled until it can be discussed at a more appropriate time. You are the one the team expects to be levelheaded. Don't disappoint them.

Despite your best efforts, however, you'll find that some folks are just not open to agreement. If you've tried everything and are still at your wits' end, sit down with the project sponsor and share your misgivings. He or she may have seen this person's behavior on other projects and are not surprised. In fact, the sponsor could possibly share ways in which you could improve the relationship.

If you witness such a blow up between team members, do your best to calm the parties. Your job is to move the project forward, so you cannot allow these types of events to disarm your authority. You don't have that much as it is!

I was in a meeting once where the manager was so feared and so abrasive that one team member broke down and cried — and his tirade wasn't even directed at her. Suffice it to say that somebody in the group reported him to human resources over the incident and believe me, he got the message.

Personal conflicts have no place on a project. They slow productivity, distract attention from the goal, and put a bad taste in everyone's mouth. Learning to tread lightly with team members is one of the keys that will get you to closing.

Company vs. Client

You would think that this type of scenario would never happen, especially because everything you've ever learned about the PM role boils down to satisfying the client. But sadly it does occur, and more often than it should. It usually starts with a misunderstanding over requirements. Say, for example, that the client requested a wish list of 700 requirements, and after the final statement of work (SOW), they were whittled down to 25. Disappointing? Sure. Realistic? Absolutely. Acceptable? Probably not and therein lies the rub.

If the requirements-gathering stage of projects were more clearly explained to the client, a flurry of subsequent disappointments could be averted. But instead, folks are mad at each other before you've even gotten passed the planning phase.

As a PM on technology projects, you are usually hired by the IT department to assist in managing the early stages of the project. This is a major problem because the client automatically assumes that you do not represent his or her interests. It's like buying a house and using the seller's realtor. You know from the start that you're going to pay more and gain less than you would if you hired your own guy. Think how the client must feel. Who will speak up for him when the testing is incomplete, dev cycles take too long, or the end product was nothing like what had been envisioned?

To curtail any feelings of doubt, you must take definitive steps to make the client feel protected. Sometimes the business analyst fills this role, which is not good because they need the freedom to focus on the requirements and testing.

What the client really needs is for the project leader to take a leadership role, stroking the stakeholders and making sure their wishes are conveyed in the manner they expect and deserve. A great example of stakeholder "stroking" emerged from the 2006 highway and metro rail project in Denver, Colorado, known as T-REX.

T-REX was the acronym for Transportation Expansion Project, a joint effort of the Colorado Department of Transportation and the Rail Transportation Department. I mention this project because, not only did the seven-year, $1.7 billion, multimodal effort come in under budget and ahead of schedule, the contractor — Southeast Corridor Constructors (SECC) — went out of its way to ensure stakeholder satisfaction. The goal was to ensure that the public was not inconvenienced during the construction work because, as most of us know, if such a project does not get public buy-in, it will be viewed as a failure, no matter what improvements result.

According to the 2003 T-REX fact book, SECC set up the following communication vehicles and risk mitigation to minimize resident angst:

- 24-hour call centers to report excessive noise and dust complaints.
- Bi-weekly newsletters.
- Presentations to homeowner associations and local employers.
- An interactive project website with real-time stats on construction areas and congestion spots.
- Additional lanes for high-occupancy vehicles to assist in getting residents around town. Lanes were never closed during construction.

This attention to the needs of its stakeholders earned the project team the Marvin M. Black Excellence in Partnering Award from the Associated General Contractors of America, which celebrates the success of stakeholders in teambuilding, improving communication, and delivering superior project quality (Spragins, 2007).

Sadly, when left solely to the project PM, successes such as this are few and far between. I have always been an advocate for client-side PMs. If there's a PM on the contractor side, why not have one on the other side, too? This should not be just a functional manager standing in as a PM or an upper-level leader who's not into details. This person would bridge the gap between the client and the contractor and ensure that nothing is left to chance, allowing the stakeholders to breathe easier throughout the entire project lifecycle. I hear some good things are happening in this area at companies using agile-driven PM methodologies, of which T-REX was one. But alas, that is not the case in most companies. Show some consideration for the client and never give them the impression you belong to the other side.

Company vs. Contractor

This relationship can potentially become the most adversarial. In this scenario, we know the identity of the company. But who is the contractor? It's you! Unless you are an internal PM, this battle is all yours. Luckily, more companies are embracing the PM consultant, and that has resulted in a number of PMs trading the full-time employment ball-and-chain for self-employed status. Bravo!

But under what circumstances might the contractor-company relationship sour? One example is being set up for failure. In my time I've seen a few PMs come-and-go. I was on one project where we went through three in as many months! But I'm not going to rag on them. They were placed in positions that were beyond their control, as well as their expertise. So I don't blame them; I blame the people who hired them. Corporate life is strange at times. I would not be surprised if those poor souls were supposed to fail just so the sponsor could distract the client from the real issues and drag things on for a while. What better way for the client to lose track of their defects or change requests? A new PM means a new project plan, or for that matter a new plan altogether.

As a contractor, it's not a bad idea to find out as much as you can about a company before you start there. This sounds like common sense, but you'd be surprised how many potential employees fail to do any investigating about the hand that might feed them. If the team uses Agile techniques you better have some experience with them. If they use Prince 2, they will expect you to know it.

Being a project manager is one of the few jobs in which you will show yourself to be really *smart* or really *stupid* within your first week on the job. You just can't hide. Either you've run meetings before or you haven't. You've written business requirements or you haven't. You've used Primavera or you haven't. There is no getting around it. You're either in or you're out.

The goal here is to keep your job by shaking any "outsider" impressions of you the project team may develop. To do that, you need to hit the ground running, know your stuff and understand the dynamics of your environment. As we discussed in Chapter 2, you don't have to feel like you're sneaking up on them in the dark. Just use your communication skills, have lunch with a few key players and keep your ear to the ground. In a word, be *resourceful*.

These days, when jobs are so hard to get and keep, you don't want to fall victim to the us-versus-them mentality. Remain as neutral as you can and do your best to get the job done.

Action Items

✔ **Be aware of potential strife-inducing scenarios** that could derail your project.

✔ **Be careful not to indulge in an us-versus-them** mentality, no matter how close you may have gotten to team members, the sponsor, the client or any other stakeholder. You are not there to make friends, you are there to successfully run the project.

✔ **Keep an eye out** for any forms of internal strife between team members, and do what you can to squelch it.

✔ **Keep the clients' best interest in mind** and work to ensure they get what they want. It may sound cliché, but the customer is always right. Try to develop some innovative ways to keep them informed and supportive.

✔ **Do not take any disagreements personally**; always take the high road.

✔ **Learn** as much as you can about the company before you take the job, then work within the accepted parameters.

Attitudes and Agendas

Real World Advice:
"Remember: you cannot always control the actions of others.
You can control only your reaction to them."
– J.N., Mobile Communications

The project hadn't even begun before Lisa started in. "Don't go with XYZ company," she warned. "They have awful customer service." Two weeks later, Jeffrey chimes in, "I heard you went with XYZ. What a big mistake that was. They can't do anything right." Then nine months into the project, the president of the company has his say: "Congratulations to the team that chose XYZ. We were a bit hesitant at first, but our project manager handled everything so well that we are getting accolades from all our customers! Job well done."

The moral of this story: negativity-toting team members can bring any project to its knees. Likely you've had some experience with them. How do you prevent them from spreading their message of doom and gloom to your project? How do you keep them from ruining things before the project gets off the ground?

Your first inclination may be to keep their input to a minimum. You may reason that if you close them out you won't have to hear about their lack of enthusiasm. But that's not reality. There will always be someone on the project who wants nothing more than to see it fail. There are a million reasons for this behavior, but the most common one is having a lack of input. In this chapter, we will examine seven behavioral types you will likely confront between the initiation and closing of a project.

Naysayers

A naysayer has a need to lead, but feels no one is giving him the chance. He may believe he has some great ideas for the project that are not getting any attention. He's like the kid on the baseball field who wants to play but would rather be asked than to volunteer. Then when he's not chosen, he proceeds to say all the other boys stink. In short, he's feeling left out.

On the job, he wants to sit on special committees and be consulted on important decisions. He wants others to value him and come to him for answers. So to get back at his perceived ignorers, he sets himself up as a prophet, proclaiming the end before it comes. It's a technique that affirms him. In his mind, it gives him power in a situation where he clearly has none.

His behavior is even more pronounced if he's seen similar projects fail. Armed with what he considers concrete evidence, he may think he is actually helping you by sharing something he knows that you don't. It's a morbid form of risk management presented in an unproductive way. His behavior sounds childish, but dissatisfied adults often betray their inner child when they feel unappreciated.

The best way to handle naysayers is to disarm them. For instance, because he thinks his information is so valuable, ask the naysayer to present his doubts in the form of a lessons-learned artifact, explaining to him that you welcome documented information to mitigate potential risks. Thank him for bringing it up, and then be on your way. One of two things will happen: Either he will provide the artifact and truly show some concern about the project's outcome, or you won't hear from him again on the subject, meaning he had no concrete evidence and just wanted to raise your blood pressure.

The interesting thing about naysayers is that once the project is off and running and people they respect are on board, they have an amazing way of forgetting that they ever complained about it. Don't fret! Just chalk it up to their inner child.

Despite the heartburn it can cause, criticism is something you should welcome on your projects because alternative ideas can spawn better approaches.

Woe-Is-Me

Ever work with someone who is very productive and a real multi-tasker, yet they complain the whole time? That is the definition of a "woe-is-me" type, which I will refer to as WIM. These people are notorious for getting all kinds of work done while fussing about having to do it. I have to admit that I am a WIM. Not all the time, but when I am working on projects at home, my husband says I never stop complaining. Why do I do it? For the very reason most WIMs complain: I'm a complainer! The rationale is that it makes me feel good knowing I am being productive, and I want others to know all the work that I am doing. Complaining about it gets the word out, and allows me to proclaim my joy at being extremely busy. I know it makes absolutely no sense, but it's the truth. I love to complain. When WIMs are complaining, they are at their happiest. When they stop complaining, something is really wrong.

There are several types of WIMs. I consider mine to be the good kind. On the other hand, you may encounter those who need a different manner of affirmation. They are the ones who never seem to get over the hump. They can't overcome any of their project obstacles and, rather than take advice, they just want to gripe. Like good WIMs, they are multi-taskers, but instead of finding joy in it, they hate it. They want someone to do their work for them, to ease their burden, to treat them special. When managing this type of WIM, I would advise you to tread lightly. I once worked with a WIM who was what you might call "old school." She was not flexible and felt things should be done the way she did them at her old job. Change was not her friend, and even the slightest adjustment to her work habits brought out the worst in her. Whenever I am in meetings with WIMs like this, I follow the LSC rule: Listen, Smile and Comfort.

First, I let them get all the griping out without interruption. All the time I am smiling, showing them that I am truly listening. I nod from time to time for emphasis. Then I proceed to comfort them by showing empathy with their situation. I share a few experiences that parallel theirs and tell them I wish things were different, too. Then I change the subject to something they may find pleasant while I escort them out of my office. The result: they are content and can go on with their day knowing someone understands.

Others are not dismissed so easily and actually need you to move obstacles out of their way. So give them a task that is attainable, something in which they can see the possibility of a good outcome. Many times, they are just feeling overwhelmed. They can't see beyond the mound of work that sits in front of them.

I have a relative who I believe is a WIM. I was staying with her for a month or so while I had my house built. She liked to collect things and had a hard time parting with items as a result. I wouldn't consider her a hoarder, but she was getting close. Anyway, when you walked into her living room (which was not that big to begin with) you would encounter mounds of paper, magazines and other stuff just lying in the middle of the floor. After a while it progressed, spreading to each end of the floor and against every wall. Finally I just said, "Why don't we clean this up?" She looked at me like I had just killed her cat. "I can't," she replied. "It's just too much." Immediately, I could see the tears filling her eyes; it was truly a heartbreaking sight. She was obviously overwhelmed at just the thought of the task and had no earthly idea of where to start.

I suggested that we compartmentalize. I volunteered to start with organizing the magazines, and she could start on the other side of the room with the newspapers. That seemed to work because now the task was broken down into manageable pieces.

The same is true of tasks you give to your WIM team members, help them to see the light at the end of the tunnel, and they will be eternally grateful.

The Half-Empty Type

Of all the behavioral types I have worked with or managed throughout my career, I have to say that the "half-empty" type tests my patience the most. I have never been able to understand why some people look at everything in a negative light. In their minds, nothing is ever right. Nothing ever works. No one is on the up and up. How can someone live life buried in 24/7 pessimism? *Just shoot me and put me out of my misery!* That's the way I feel whenever I'm around them.

This attitude is depressing and completely unfounded in 99.9 percent of all cases. On a project team, you want to be aware of these false contributors. Similar to the naysayers, the half-empty team member is jaded by past experience. Some former event or situation affected them so badly that they never got over it and so everything that follows is presumed to end with the same result. It's sad, really.

Your first inclination will be to pull them out of the funk, but the reality is they have to *want* to get out. Most of the time they don't. Or can't. It's not your job as the PM to be their personal therapist, but it is your job to ensure their pessimistic attitude does not permeate the rest of the team.

I read a great article entitled "The Real Reason People Won't Change" by Robert Kegan and Lisa Laskow Lahey, two researchers whose aim was to get to the bottom of why some people are resistant to change. Their theory is that there is a psychological dynamic called "competing commitment" that prevents some of us from tapping into the underlying reasons for an aversion to something new. They say that if we take the time to perform an honest assessment, we will find the reason behind our resistance. It's actually very powerful stuff. The challenge is getting your team members to take the assessment and to be honest in their answers.

Their "competing commitment" could be anything from a hang-up about being different than their peer group to a fear of failure. Here are a few examples I've condensed from the authors' research:

- John, as the only African-American on an otherwise all-white executive team, held back from total immersion due to a competing commitment not to become "too white."

- Helen's competing commitment to remain Andrew's subordinate caused her to underperform once promoted to his level. Becoming his peer was a role she was not comfortable taking on.

Attempting to understand is the first step to getting over these dysfunctional behaviors in the workplace. As a PM consultant, there is little you can do except find a way to work around them. However, if you are a full-time employee, it might be a good idea to bring this kind of assessment to the attention of your training department. Any exercise that can assist in keeping the project on track should be examined.

Getting back to the half-empty type, there are other ways to get around all the negativity and to keep it from souring the team. First, schedule a one-on-one meeting with him or her and attempt to iron out the problem by using open-ended rather than accusatory questions. This way you can get down to the brass tacks of their issues. Even if he is voicing things you already know to be true, avoid buying into his lack of optimism. As the PM, you are already likely to be mitigating problems, so continue to take the high road and promote the positive. Help the team member to realize that there is little to be gained by putting a dark face on an already unpleasant situation. Encourage him to be a champion of the cause so that others who may also be feeling discouraged don't become unproductive. That would only make the issue drag on even longer and put the entire project in jeopardy.

There is no miracle cure or single answer for getting passed these divisive personality traits. The best you can do is recognize them when they are presented and learn to manage them. I had an experience with one such personality, and I have to admit that it was hard for me to keep my composure. I had to really resist the urge to retaliate or start a confrontation. Nowadays, I take a deep breath before responding, and then I pretend my name is Mark.

Let me explain.

Years ago I worked for a guy who had the gift of diplomacy in the workplace. You guessed it. His name was Mark.

Mark could sit patiently through a tirade from a coworker with his legs crossed, his eyes firmly fixed on his nemesis, and a smile on his face. Make no mistake, he was fuming inside, but you couldn't tell. That was the beauty of Mark's style. "Never let 'em see ya sweat," he'd always say.

One day in particular, we were in his office talking to a producer. She was going on and on about why the approach we had proposed to take on an upcoming project was just not going to work. In his usual calming way, Mark sat there and listened. But this time I knew she was dead wrong, and I wanted him to agree with me. He didn't! In fact, he kept telling me to pipe down as he continued to show her sympathy and understanding. I was silent but livid. And unlike Mark, it showed. I could not believe he was allowing her to lead him down the primrose path, when I knew he didn't agree with a word she was saying.

After she left, I shut the door and proceeded to question his actions. He apologized for discounting me during the meeting. He figured I could take the treatment of being dismissed, based on what he knew about my personality. I learned later that it was all part of his strategy.

He needed her on board, so he had no choice but to appease her. He did what she wanted: he heard her out. After that day, I took that strategy and learned to apply it in similar situations. It became my Listen, Smile and Comfort approach.

The bottom line is that when you need someone and you know pushing back is going to yield no results, the only alternative is to listen. Now let's look at behaviors that tend to be less adverse but, at the same time, a hindrance to project success:

The All-Over-Its

The all-over-its are your team members who act too quickly, thinking they know what you want them to do before the assignment is fully communicated.

These are the ones who also have a tendency to cut you off in mid-sentence. It's not that they don't respect you, to the contrary. They are trying to let you know they have already anticipated your every need. In their own peculiar way, they are attempting to be helpful.

This behavior, while pretty annoying to some, betrays a willingness to become indispensable. They think this behavior will show you how on top of things they are.

The best way to handle someone with this quirk is to be patient. Obviously, you can't talk at the same time, so be the more professional half of this dueling duet and allow him to express what he thinks you mean. After he is finished, simply say, "OK, now let me explain what I really need. While I'm doing that, why don't you just take notes and listen? That way you can be sure to capture all the details."

This comment, while disarming, is not meant to be delivered with a snotty tone or any hint of condescension. Just say it and be done with it. You might smile while saying it. That adds a nice touch.

Here is why I suggest this approach: If you can establish a precedent early on, you can avoid the fate that usually befalls managers who allow this behavior to continue unchecked. The all-over-its can use your lack of a detailed explanation against you. For example, let's say you had a task and, before fully explaining it, the team member who has this habit convinces you he knows what to do. He goes off and he does something. Trouble is it's not what you wanted. The result: He blames you rather than recognize it was his desire to rush ahead that created the mess. Be clear early and often if you are managing an all-over-it behavior type.

Over-Pleasers

Over-pleasers are similar to all-over-its with one distinct difference: they do not anticipate anything. These people wait for you to tell them what you want; their goal is to make it happen.

Such team members are often referred to as butt-kissers, yet some of them are so sincere that you almost feel sorry for them. After all, they are only trying to do the best job they possibly can, right?

Maybe.

The over-pleaser, as you have probably surmised by now, has an agenda, just like anyone else. In this case, it could be job security. If the over-pleaser does everything you tell him to do — to the letter — there is no one to blame but you if things pertaining to the project go astray. This person is doing not only your bidding, but it's likely that he's also doing the bidding of the person in power above you. Think about it. If your boss asked him what happened, what do you think he's going to say? "I was only doing what the project manager told me to do." The trade-off for appeasing an over-pleaser is accepting the good along with the bad.

Knowledge-Hoarders

I used to love watching old silent comedies. It seemed there was always a character who would drop a banana peel at the precise moment that another character was walking by. After the unsuspecting victim fell flat on his backside, inevitably, the punch line would be, "Oops, sorry about that."

That basically sums up the modus operandi of the knowledge-hoarder.

Though they bear no resemblance to the pathetic junk collectors in the world, these hoarders can create just as much disorder. They have the uncanny ability to withhold crucial information at the most inopportune times.

What the knowledge-hoarder desires is power. As the saying goes, "information is the modern commodity," and they believe this with conviction. If they possess something you need, they rationalize that you will be willing to pay dearly for it. Sometimes it's done in exchange for a favor. Other times it's done out of a desire to see you hang. The latter should give you the most concern because your project could be jeopardized as a result.

Managing the knowledge-hoarder is most difficult when that person is a key stakeholder and in a position to affect the time and scope of the project. To avoid all-out war, it would be to your advantage to find an alternative source from among your remaining stakeholders. If that means going over this person's head, I suggest you do so only after you have exhausted all other possibilities, such as by consulting with a peer within this person's department or someone else on the team in a position to know or have access to the information.

Info-tainers

Did you ever meet someone at a professional function who finishes the telling of another person's recollections? For example, a person is recounting a news report relating to an unusual event that took place, and before she has a chance to divulge the most interesting part, another person chimes in, delivering the golden nugget. Not only that, this person takes over the storytelling and finishes up with one or two other things relating to that story you might also like to know. You've just met an Info-tainer.

Info-tainers like to impress the team with what they know. In fact, they need to know that you know they know something. You can easily detect when an info-tainer is in your midst. Once a subject is raised that she knows about, she's out the gate and down to the homestretch. She will even throw out all kinds of additional information to circumvent the possibility of anyone else mentioning it. It's important for info-tainers to be accepted as the keepers of the latest. Doesn't matter what it is; if it's new and it could affect you, she knows it.

Info-tainers are usually harmless in relation to your project's success and many times they can be quite helpful; especially if you also have a knowledge-hoarder on the stakeholder list.

Action Items

- When confronted with negativism that threatens to affect your project, get to the heart of the matter by:

    1. Examining the motivation behind the attitude.

    2. Determining an action plan to disarm it.

    3. Turning the situation around to work in your favor.

- Read a few articles that provide examples on how to manage difficult people. The Harvard Business Review is a good place to start.

- Never let the person bringing negativity cause you to retaliate in kind. As Mark says, "Never let 'em see ya sweat."

- As an exercise to prepare for negative behaviors, investigate whether the company offers workshops on managing people. If you are a contractor, your local Project Management Institute chapter may also be able to provide helpful resources.

- Use tact, patience and discernment with less negative behavior types. Find creative ways to deflect their agendas before they penetrate the project atmosphere.

Office Politics

Real World Advice:
"Be positive and try to understand the root cause of the
conflict before trying to come up with solutions."
— Anonymous, Insurance Industry

If you've been in the workplace for some time, you know that office politics often determine how you are received, how your views are perceived, and how many rungs of the corporate ladder you're able to successfully negotiate over the life of your professional career. It's a dirty term, but one everyone has to acknowledge. Your view of office politics may depend on how willing you are to "play the game." And sadly, it is a game. So ask yourself these questions: How can I recognize what politics are playing out in my work environment? What do I need to know about them in order to keep my project on track?

Because office politics can manifest itself differently — depending on the company, the atmosphere and the people — getting answers may be difficult. First, let's begin with a definition to help you focus your research. Office politics is nothing more than *people attempting to influence other people to their way of thinking*, whether it's by way of the rumor mill, by skillful alignment with department power brokers, by manipulation, or by just doing a darn good job and knowing how to get the word out about it.

If you don't consider these activities to be politics, it could explain why you don't recognize it when it happens. If you are doing — or have done — some of these actions, you are playing politics, albeit unknowingly.

Influence can take many forms, so let's examine a few of them. As we do so, take note of any that you have noticed in your own environment. You may be surprised that you did not conceive of them as politics.

The Perp Walk

Each of us has been in a situation in which we made a mistake during a project. We may have misspoken about a particular fact, or perhaps we sent out incorrect information regarding a deliverable. Unfortunately, there is always someone on the project who notices and feels compelled to make sure others notice it, too. I refer to this as the perp walk. You know this term; it's the act of taking a prisoner from the jailhouse to the courthouse, handcuffed and dressed in the orange clown suit. Law enforcement officers put the perp (or perpetrator) through this ordeal as a form of humiliation because it's an opportunity to make the justice system look good and an injustice look bad.

When team members on your project broadcast your mistakes to others, this is a form of perp walk. They want to humiliate you. They may want others to perceive you as incompetent. Maybe they want your job, or possibly you inadvertently did something to them and they are paying you back. Whatever the reason behind it, the perp walk is a form of office politics and, unless you are perfect in all your actions, this is one political maneuver you may not be able to avoid. However, it is important how you respond to the humiliation. This will ultimately determine whether the real perpetrators are successful or whether they are shown up for their lack of couth. Don't take their behavior to heart; as I said, no one is perfect. Even the person causing your pain will at some point fall victim to a mistake. In that case, don't return evil for evil. Show that you are above such petty nonsense and overlook the error. The result is in your control, so be aware and be tactful.

Silent Condemnation

Have you ever been in a meeting defending your point of view on a matter and, as you are explaining yourself, observed the reactions of others? According to psychologist Gary Wells, "We look for cues in our environment to decide what's an appropriate answer, what's an appropriate response. That's human nature."

He is referring to nonverbal communication that indicates either approval or disapproval in the form of facial expressions, fidgeting or other clues. Wells looks at these subtleties in some very serious studies. He is a professor at Iowa State University, and his subject is police lineups. Wells has surmised that during photo ID sessions, in which the victim views pictures of suspects, the officer may unknowingly influence him to make the wrong identification. This, Wells says, often results in an innocent person being convicted.

In an interview with National Public Radio's Alix Spiegel, Wells explained that small changes in posture or speech by the officer can cause the victim to second-guess his memory of the suspect, leading him to unintentionally finger the wrong person.

As you observe the silent communication of your team members, stakeholders or clients, keep in mind that these nuances may actually be unconscious and have absolutely nothing to do with anything you are saying. In fact, one Dallas police officer who was also interviewed by NPR said his officers were not even aware they were making gestures that could be considered influential. The lesson for you, as a PM, is to not take your cues from your audience, especially if you come to the meeting prepared. Have your facts straight and be confident that your proposal is rock solid. Otherwise, someone listening with the intent to derail your ideas will be successful; you will be playing into his hands and thus become a victim of office politics. Don't give him the satisfaction.

Unacknowledged Contributions

For many, recognition is the best reward for a good day's work. It makes all the mess and frustration it took to get there somehow worthwhile. So imagine someone else denying you that acknowledgment just because he can.

I hate to break it to you, but as a PM, more often than not, you may find yourself in that situation because you are in a position that typically brings with it little real authority. Sure you are laden with a ton of responsibility and accountability, but in most cases you still have to gain approval for just about everything you do. You cannot afford to be concerned when your contributions are discounted, ignored or even stolen by your sponsor or another project lead. It is better to allow someone else to get the credit as long as the thing gets done. Always recognize that — no matter what — it's all about the project and not about you.

I've had several supervisors who blatantly took credit for my ideas in public settings. But I was fine with that because it showed me two things: 1) the idea was good, and 2) my services were needed. That is all I am there for — to get the project from A to Z. If I accomplished that goal, I've gotten all of the recognition I need. It's best to keep silent, smile and take it in stride. A supervisor taking credit for the work of subordinates is an age-old business practice, so don't take it personally. After all, there are many poor saps in the corporate world who have lost much more than just the credit for a fabulous idea.

Flunky Finesse

Another form of office politics is what I call flunky finesse. The rationale is this: If there is no other way to get what you want, kiss up to the big guy and trash the competition.

This situation happened to me while I was working as a news producer. I was looking for a new job and discovered that a former colleague was the news director at a local station. He was a great guy, extremely competent and well-liked by his team. We had a good rapport at the former shop, so he hired me for an open slot. I was not there six months before they fired my friend, and I subsequently quit. Here's why: Before I arrived at that station my friend had been promoted over the assistant news director who had been there for a while. I could tell immediately that things were not very cozy between the two of them. This person was apparently going to avenge the slight and set out to get my friend fired. He began circulating less-than-flattering status reports of newsroom performance to the general manager, who he was spending a lot of personal time with. The next thing I knew my friend was out the door. So why did I quit? I left on principle. The firing was clearly an injustice with no facts to back it up. By the way, guess who became the next news director? Office politics wins again.

Such influence takes place in countless ways every day at every job level. Getting away from office politics is probably not going to happen as long as there are people with ambition or with an ax to grind.

Harassment

Now might be a good time to remind you that the line between some forms of office politics and harassment can often blur. It's important for you as the project manager to be aware of what crosses the line. Harassment is not just sexual; race, religious and age discrimination also fall under this category. You must not only discourage any form of harassment or discrimination among your team members, but you must avoid it as well.

Some companies require employees to participate in training courses to assist them in understanding and avoiding these behaviors. Even if a company doesn't provide training, it is still required to inform employees of the law and to post the federal guidelines in break rooms or other public areas where employees gather.

Know your company's policy and follow it. If you are unsure of what the Equal Employment Opportunity Commission (EEOC) considers harassment, see the guidelines below:

"Harassment is a form of employment discrimination that violates Title VII of the Civil Rights Act of 1964, the Age Discrimination in Employment Act of 1967, (ADEA), and the Americans with Disabilities Act of 1990, (ADA)."

"Harassment is unwelcome conduct that is based on race, color, religion, sex (including pregnancy), national origin, age (40 or older), disability or genetic information. Harassment becomes unlawful where 1) enduring the offensive conduct becomes a condition of continued employment, or 2) the conduct is severe or pervasive enough to create a work environment that a reasonable person would consider intimidating, hostile, or abusive. Anti-discrimination laws also prohibit harassment against individuals in retaliation for filing a discrimination charge, testifying, or participating in any way in an investigation, proceeding,

or lawsuit under these laws; or opposing employment practices that they reasonably believe discriminate against individuals, in violation of these laws."

"Petty slights, annoyances, and isolated incidents (unless extremely serious) will not rise to the level of illegality. To be unlawful, the conduct must create a work environment that would be intimidating, hostile, or offensive to reasonable people."

"Offensive conduct may include, but is not limited to, offensive jokes, slurs, epithets or name calling, physical assaults or threats, intimidation, ridicule or mockery, insults or put-downs, offensive objects or pictures, and interference with work performance. Harassment can occur in a variety of circumstances, including, but not limited to, the following:

- *The harasser can be the victim's supervisor, a supervisor in another area, an agent of the employer, a co-worker, or a non-employee.*
- *The victim does not have to be the person harassed, but can be anyone affected by the offensive conduct.*
- *Unlawful harassment may occur without economic injury to, or discharge of, the victim." (EEOC)*

When it comes to office politics, keep in mind that no matter what you do, there will always be someone who has an ulterior motive, a hidden agenda, a beef or whatever. It's human nature. Just be sure you are prepared to address it in the most professional way necessary. Understanding your inability to control the situation, there are some basic things you can do to avoid the snare of office politics. The following action items mention just a few.

Of course, even if you remain alert, stay below the radar and get your work done, there is still a chance you could be blindsided by the sting of office politics. Take each situation as it comes. Once you've been on the job a while you will usually begin to see a pattern and can act accordingly.

Action Items

✔ **Listen to the admin.** I know this may sound strange, but the one person who knows everything is the administrative assistant or executive secretary or whatever he or she is called at your company. Think about it. Leaders come and go, but who seems to maintain longevity? There's a reason for it. They know where all the bodies are buried and that is good information for the next boss. Why let that kind of gold mine leave the office? If the admin warns you that something is going on in the organization, it's probably true.

✔ **Read 1 Thessalonians 4:11 daily.** Know what it says? *"Make it your aim to live quietly and mind your own business."* Believe it or not, the Bible actually says that. It also admonishes us not to be nosy (1 Peter 4:15). In the area of office politics, I'd say that's sound advice.

✔ **Get to know your co-workers.** Depending on your industry, this one can be tricky. Some schools of thought suggest that you lunch with co-workers, but those spending too many lunches together as a group will be labeled as a clique. Others say a few drinks after work or on the weekend is a great way to bond; then again, what you say in a seemingly relaxed setting on Saturday could end up circulating in an email on Monday. Here's what I say: You don't have to become their "bud"; just be friendly. For instance, ask about their families and so forth, but not just for the sake of getting ahead (such as complimenting your boss's kids every chance you get). Show genuine interest. This will keep you in the loop when the subject turns back to work; studies have shown that people communicate more with those they trust.

✔ **Don't start rumors or spread them.** A close second to minding your own business is avoiding the rumor mill. This has saved me on more than one occasion. I've heard things on the job that I will take to my grave. It's just not wise to engage in gossip, and it can often backfire, putting you in a bad light or, worse, the unemployment line. Again, trust is what you want to build so that you can have influence when the need arises.

Action Items

✔ Avoid harassment. Be careful what you say and what you do, or you could end up in court.

✔ Share little and observe much. Some things are just not safe to share. If you are not sure of someone's motives, keep your plans to yourself. On the other hand, being observant to what others say and do usually yields fruit. Practice active listening. Put any information you gain in the back of your mind. You may need to draw on it later.

✔ Do good work, and promote it regularly. This advice is probably the most tried and true when groping your way through the mire of office politics. Blowing your own horn is not bragging if it is done with tact. Find ways to show how your work has improved a process or functionality. Get your name in the department newsletter for the product you helped innovate. Volunteer when the boss needs someone to manage an unexpected initiative. Make your good deeds known and continue to perform. You will get noticed. Then again, if your idea is stolen, don't sweat it. At least you know where it came from.

✔ Form a board of directors. I received this advice a few years ago, and it has proven beneficial. A board of directors is simply a network of trusted colleagues, mentors or non-industry advisers who can assist you in handling issues or making choices. They can offer counsel based on their own experiences and relieve anxiety you may feel. My group met once a quarter. Some meet once a month, or whenever the organizer (you) needs help. It can be done as a group or one-on-one. Once established, you'll wonder how you ever did without it.

The 5 Ws and H

Real World Advice:
"Keep in mind that, as the PM, it is your responsibility
to control the project and everything in it."
— D.P., Information Technology

In the beginning, the only means of communication available to us was what God gave us: a voice and body language. Nowadays we can do just about everything via technology — texting, tweeting and so on. But despite these communication advances, we still miscommunicate. And sometimes we just don't communicate at all!

In fact, some of the modern convenience-driven options available for communicating are making us less communicative. That may be one reason why some employers are prohibiting the use of these tools in the workplace (we'll talk more about that later).

Sadly, many project managers view communication as simply informing others of project progress, so the medium or approach used may be given little consideration. But aside from status updates, you do a wide range of communicating to a number of people affected by your project, so your view of communication may warrant examination. That is, if you want to do a good job of managing personalities on your projects.

Here is another quiz, courtesy of Mindtools.com, to gauge your communication skills. This one is not a joke; rather, it will enable you to do a personal assessment so you can make the necessary changes to improve how you communicate with others:

	Statement	Not at all	Rarely	Some times	Often	Very Often
1	When I have a problem, I try to solve it myself before asking my boss what to do.					
2	When I delegate work, I give it to whoever has the most time available.					
3	I follow up with team members whenever I see that their behavior has a negative impact on customer service.					
4	I make decisions following careful analysis, rather than relying on gut instinct.					
5	I let my team members figure out for themselves how best to work together – teams are a work in progress!					
6	I wait before disciplining a team member, so that people have a chance to correct their behaviors for themselves.					

	Statement	Not at all	Rarely	Some times	Often	Very Often
7	Technical skills are the most important skills that I need to be an effective manager.					
8	I spend time talking with my team about what's going well and what needs improving.					
9	In meetings, I take on the role of moderator/facilitator when necessary, and I help my team reach a better understanding of the issue or reach consensus.					
10	I fully understand how the business processes in my department operate, and I'm working to eliminate bottlenecks.					
11	When putting together a team, I consider the skills I need — and then I seek people who best fit my criteria.					
12	I do all that I can to avoid conflict in my team.					
13	I try to motivate people within my team by tailoring my approach to motivation to match each individual's needs.					
14	When my team makes a significant mistake, I update my boss on what has happened, and then I think of it as an important lesson learned.					
15	When conflict occurs within a new team, I accept it as an inevitable stage in the team development process.					

(Mind Tools)

Score	Comment
20-46	You need to improve your management skills urgently. If you want to be effective in a leadership role, you must learn how to organize and monitor your team's work. Now is the time to start developing these skills to increase your team's success!
47-73	You're on your way to becoming a good manager. You're doing some things really well, and these are likely the things you feel comfortable with. Now it's time to work on the skills that you've been avoiding. Focus on the areas where your score was low, and figure out what you can do to make the improvements you need.
74-100	You're doing a great job managing your team. Now you should concentrate on improving your skills even further. In what areas did you score a bit low? That's where you can develop improvement goals. Also, think about how you can take advantage of these skills to reach your career goals.

In my experience, a lack of proper communication is usually the root cause of personality conflicts. Most of us can talk, right? But very few of us really communicate. The key is to do so accurately and appropriately.

One of the most important things I learned while pursuing my undergraduate degree in Communications was the basic communication model. My rendition of it is below:

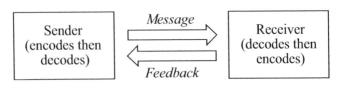

FIGURE 1: COMMUNICATION MODEL

During the course of simple communication, the sender *encodes* or "packages" the message for dissemination. Once that message gets to the receiver, he in turn *decodes* (or unpacks) it and interprets what you were trying to say. Then he encodes his response (feedback) and sends it back. The problem that often arises is that the message sent is not always the message interpreted. There is "noise" as it were, between the sender and the recipient that colors the message (or interferes with it), which can take the form of personal bias, misunderstanding, culturing differences, etc. What this model does is assist you in affecting the way you construct the message because not everyone is going to receive the message in the same way or perceive the same intent.

Remember that communication is not limited to just words. For instance, if you manage a virtual team, you may never see your team members in person. You can't read their body language or see how they respond to your messages. In addition, keeping in touch with offshore project members may present language and time-zone barriers that can further add to communication challenges. So let's review both direct and indirect communication methods and see where we can find room for improvement.

Direct Messaging

Face-to-face, email, phone calls, video conferencing and instant messages are all forms of direct communication. These are the forms you likely will use during your project. By means of these tools, you are usually communicating the "what" of your project. But "what" is not the only piece of information you must get across to your audiences.

That's where the 5 Ws and H come in.

For those of us in the writing professions — and especially those who got their start in a news organization —"the 5 Ws and H" are the basics, the foundation of news gathering. It is a term that is etched into the collective memory of every journalism student, past and present.

The 5 Ws and H are *who, what, when, where, why* and *how*.

As a project manager, this basic tenet of communication is an excellent example to follow. No matter which medium is used, don't lay a finger on that keyboard (or touchpad) until you've asked yourself these questions:

Who does this relate to?
What is the information about?
When did it happen (or is it happening)?
Where did this take place (or is it taking place)?
Why are you communicating this?
How does the recipient need to react?

Confining your communication to the "what" will get you limited results. The needs of every individual who receives your communication should be considered. For example, the project sponsor may need to know *how* to respond to this information; in other words, what do you need them to do? And *why* do they need to do it? You may tell the client that you missed a milestone, but they will also need to know *why* as well as *when* will the deliverable happen so they can plan accordingly. Keeping in mind what your recipients need from your communication will help them to get their own jobs done. In fact, why not ask them how they prefer to receive communication and what information they need in it? This will eliminate any guesswork.

For example, the client may need only a bi-weekly update on the status of deliverables. This can be done during a conference call or on-site visit. I would not recommend choosing email for this audience, unless they are internal and could not make a meeting or a call. It's too impersonal. Sending an instant message (IM) is considered unprofessional and so would be out of the question at most firms.

Sponsors usually need high-level information on how the project is progressing, minus the dirty details. Unless an escalation is needed, this is usually all the communication they want.

Other stakeholders, such as those who will use the finished product, may not hear anything about the project until it's time to plan the deployment. At that time, you'll provide communication on when the release will launch, what training will be provided, and so on. In some cases, user-testing may take place with a select group of stakeholders prior to deployment. You will likely communicate this information weeks in advance through email, a meeting, a conference call or an on-site visit.

For this group, you'll want to follow the advice I received in my freshman creative writing class: Assume the reader knows nothing. Even though you have been living and breathing this project for months — maybe even years

— the end user has not; so don't forget the basics when communicating to these stakeholders. Simple but detailed is the best approach.

If your communication matrix includes a marketing group or public relations team, your goal is to convince them to sell the features and benefits of your project deliverables to their customers. Put on your sales cap and create communication in their language, so they will be pumped about the product and reflect that in their external messaging.

If you take the time to consider what you have to communicate, to whom, and how you should do it, based on the recipient's needs, you will greatly improve your ability to manage the varied personalities on your projects.

The Need-to-Know Factor

Are there cases when you don't tell all? Is there a method of delivering only part of the story without violating your professional ethics? The answer to both questions is yes. However, this type of communication can be tricky because it requires a balance between transparency and what I call the "need-to-know factor."

A classic and tragic example of applying this method the *wrong* way was the Space Shuttle Challenger disaster in 1986. Crucial information regarding the ability of the O ring seals in the rocket boosters to withstand the cold temps that morning was not communicated up the chain of command as far as it needed to go, and those who were in a position to advance it refused to do so. These actions were due not only to a lack of communication, but also to an intentional withholding of known information. Why? Fear was one reason. No one likes to be the bearer of bad news. But those who did attempt to get the information to the right people were stifled by others who did not want to admit that anything was wrong.

The lesson for you is this: Saving face is not worth the avalanche of problems that are sure to follow by not communicating. The eight people on that shuttle may not have died had a decision been made to scrub the launch in favor of investigating the repeatedly reported difficulty. But their concern was not the lives of people; rather, it was what the media would think of yet another canceled launch. Essentially, reputation was of paramount importance. As it turned out, their actions did nothing to save their personal reputations, and it certainly was no boost to the space program. In fact, that incident is recorded as the worst in NASA's history, and everyone involved is remembered right along with it.

So much for saving face.

Now let's look at a good example of the need-to-know factor, using a project risk scenario as our test communiqué. The scenario goes like this: A deliverable that IT had expected to complete in six days with no lag time has dragged on for nearly two weeks. The client is expecting to review the deliverable during the next gate check and either sign off or reject it. No one is aware of this delay except you, the IT manager, the developers working on it and quality control. Everyone in this group has agreed the deliverable can be completed before the next gate check, which is three weeks away; however, the scope creep this delay caused will likely put other deliverables in jeopardy. Your job is to create a communication to all those who *need to know* this information.

So, then, who needs to know?

The client? No. Clients do not need this level of detail at this point. There is a possibility that the scope creep can be corrected. There is no need to cause undo anxiety while there is still hope. Perform some resource leveling, crash the project, get approval to hire some temps. Do whatever you can do to get things back on track before resorting to communicating with the client. Once you have exhausted your options and you do have to inform them, you will at least have an action plan to bring to the table, having first taken all necessary steps to correct the issue.

The sponsor? Yes. The sponsor is likely the one who hired you and you never want them to be in the dark; otherwise, they can't help you if you get into a bind. On the other hand, if you were hired by IT, do not communicate with the sponsor unless you are required to give regular updates to leadership. In that case, save it for the next status meeting. As mentioned, with proper planning, the issue will likely have been corrected by then.

In fact, besides you and the group working on the deliverable, no one else needs to know about this right now. You should be getting regular updates on development, so simply give them a reasonable deadline for mitigation and forego the communication for the moment. Granted, this is just an example. A myriad of extenuating circumstances might come into play if this were a real situation; in that case, you would have to weigh all the issues before making a final determination on when and to whom you should communicate. But no matter what you do, DON'T LIE. If you ever get to a place where you cannot tell the truth, you and your project need some serious course correction.

While you can't plan for everything, you can develop some kind of attack strategy using risk management. No doubt you are familiar with the *knowns* and *unknowns* used in risk assessment:

Known knowns describe issues you can identify. To some degree you can even calculate the likelihood of their taking place.

Known unknowns describe issues you can also identify, but you're not currently able to calculate the likelihood of their taking place.

Unknown unknowns describe issues you cannot identify nor are you able to calculate the likelihood they will take place (the fewer you have of these the better).

After documenting these with your team and anyone else who has valuable input, start figuring out how to respond in the event one of these issues develops.

Using this method at least gives you a fighting chance when risky situations arise. It's called Plan B and trust me, every PM needs one. Once you have yours, you can communicate your "need to know" news more confidently and completely.

Cross-cultural Awareness and Communication

In 2010, the Bureau of Labor Statistics predicted that, by 2018, our American workforce would increase by 10 percent, with racially and ethnically diverse employees making up most of that number. I have recently been privileged to work with more colleagues from other countries — from Iran, India, Poland, Mexico and Denmark, to name just a few — than I have in my entire career.

As you work with a more diverse team, differences in culture will manifest themselves in a number of ways. For me, language has been the most prominent concern. I sometimes find it difficult to understand American English as it is spoken by a non-native. This is a problem particularly over the phone or during video conferencing. If this is an issue for you, I suggest providing a chat component so the speaker who is misunderstood can type his or her response. Don't be embarrassed to politely interrupt and ask that something either be repeated or provided in written form. It is better to ask than to misinterpret the message. Most people will understand and be happy to slow down and repeat a comment or send it in writing.

If you are an alien resident in another country, try not to react negatively if someone does not understand your pronunciation of the native language. Ask if what you are saying is being understood and make attempts at clarity whenever you can. Your listeners will appreciate your desire to communicate effectively with them.

In addition, team members who are located in different time zones will appreciate meetings, messages or calls that take place during their regular work hours, so they have the appropriate amount of time to respond. Be accommodating when possible and any communication from you will be well received.

Possessed with these abilities, the belief is that managers can more effectively anticipate potential problems within teams and handle them with more compassion and empathy.

Action Items

✔ Think about your audience before you create any communication, then determine how to proceed.

✔ Follow the 5 Ws and H in crafting a message:

Who?
What?
When?
Where?
Why?
How?

✔ **Know the acceptable mediums of communication** in your particular workplace. Is an instant message appropriate, and if so, when?

Action Items

✓ **Be aware of cultural differences** that could affect the way your message is received and work hard to avoid offending the recipient.

✓ **Be clear in your communication** or not everyone will interpret the message the way you intend it.

✓ Ensure you **do not omit any stakeholders** in your communication before, during or after the project. Create a communication matrix and follow it.

✓ **Know what forms of communication** are needed by asking your sponsor how they prefer to receive it, such as in status updates or escalations.

✓ **Evaluate yourself** as a communicator using the self-assessment on page 78 then make any necessary changes.

✓ **Be courteous**. Back in the 1870s there was a saying, "Courtesy is the politeness of kings." Why not display your royal highness rather than taking the low road?

Indirect Messaging

Real World Advice:
"Try to see beyond the obvious and get to the meat of the issue."
— T.K., Web Development

So far, we've only discussed formal communication. Now let's look at some less obvious forms of communicating that also need consideration.

Another form of communication you will encounter on your projects is known as *indirect messaging*. It is meant not just to inform, but also to convey intentions, feelings and even warnings. Indirect messaging can sometimes be missed. Recognizing the methods when confronted with them will help you process the information and maneuver potentially dangerous waters. Yes, some forms of communication are intentionally meant to cause harm to you and the project, so be on the lookout.

We'll review four examples of such messaging: cursory responses, counter-framing, planting and negative feedback.

These and other such artfully contrived ways to get a

point across are tools used by your boss, your team members and your stakeholders. Maybe you use them, too. The examples in this chapter will teach you how to decipher the messages as well as help you discern the intent of the messenger.

Cursory Responses

In your own observations, I'm sure you've picked up on some forms of indirect communication such as facial expressions and other forms of body language. These can say a lot about a person. But be aware that some people use these subtle forms of indirect communication to intentionally send a message.

In college, when I took an organizational behavior course, I remember one classroom example in which the professor explained that, when you are talking to a person and they keep nodding their head in agreement, it is a form of active listening. But nodding can also mean the listener is projecting a *cursory response* to your conversation. Used in this context, nodding the head is just a pretense. The person doesn't agree with you. She isn't even listening. What she would really like to do is get you out of her office. If you've been observant in previous dealings with a person, you should be able to distinguish the intent.

This method is used quite a bit by upper-level managers who have multiple direct reports. If you are a victim of the continuous nod, take the hint and cut the conversation short. If you must get an approval or some other important item from this person, state your case at the outset and don't linger after the transaction is complete. I guarantee that you will win points with this person because you recognize their need to get on to something more pressing. Maybe the next time they will give you more of their attention.

Counter-framing

Counter-framing is a subtlety I have yet to master but continue to work on. It's used when the messenger needs to convey not-so-good news and is forced to resort to packaging it so that your perception (or frame) is reversed or changed to the way he or she would like you to view it.

For instance, let's say your boss needs someone to train the new senior project manager, but he can't ask you to do it because he knows you will take issue with training someone for a job you applied for and rightly deserved. If he bluntly says, "I want you to train this person," he knows your framing of the conversation will lead you to deduce that he is using you and conclude that he devalues you and could eventually fire you. Instead, he comes up with a way to communicate this task to make it more palatable to you.

He attempts to *counter-frame* it by telling you the new person likely won't last a week and appears to be a slow learner — unlike you, his best PM. He proceeds to melt you down by complimenting your past achievements and quick study abilities. He is reassuring, saying that most of the good projects will have to be managed by you until this person can get up to speed, if that ever happens. He may even blame someone else for making him hire the guy. If he successfully sells you on the idea, you walk away feeling empowered, and he has his knowledge-transfer completed.

Granted, some who try this technique are easy to see through. But beware the skilled counter-framer! He will have you doing things you had no intention of doing, and you'll walk out of his office wondering what just happened.

On the other hand, counter-framing can be useful to you, especially if you are working in an agile project environment. In the agile "bullpen," you are often rubbing shoulders with a condensed version of the entire project team, including your stakeholders. Despite all that is said about the transparency and collaboration of the agile approach, at the end of the day, you are still managing two opposing agendas: the client's and IT's. In this case, your project communication is in desperate need of a good counter-framer.

Planting

This form of indirect messaging is used when someone wants to relay an idea — or falsehood — without actually conveying the message directly to the intended person or group.

You may have practiced this form of indirect communication in grade school. Remember when you liked a girl or boy but didn't want to tell her or him yourself? You sent a friend to find out if that person also liked you by asking probing questions. Your friend was a plant, a way for you to avoid direct communication with the object of your affection.

Planting that occurs during projects works the same way. For example, you are in your office listening in on a conference call when the moderator begins to make intentionally untrue statements about a project decision. He has had a beef against you for months. You know the correct information was delivered in an earlier meeting that the moderator's boss attended. What do you do? You were not invited to the call, so chiming in is not an option.

Your boss is not on the call, but you need to assure him that these statements are incorrect before he gets wind of what is going on. You decide to send an instant message to the moderator's boss because he is also not on the call. You ask for a reiteration of the correct information discussed in the morning meeting. He confirms your side of things, not knowing that his employee is communicating incorrect information. You now send the instant message to your boss (and yourself) as leverage. He then questions the moderator's boss about the information, which redeems you. *Planting* allows you to avoid making a big deal of the error on the call and lowering yourself to the moderator's level. Instead, you've just sent an indirect message to the moderator by way of his boss, who handily corrects his employee the next day.

Negative Feedback

From time to time, nerves are set on edge and people will say and do things out of frustration. This is particularly true on projects where team members must work closely together for long periods of time. Under such circumstances, incorrect forms of discipline may take place. Negative feedback is a method of indirect messaging that can come from anyone, but is usually employed by a supervisor or other authority figure in an attempt to change a subordinate's behavior.

In this form of communication, you may find yourself the victim of "bad press," as I like to call it. For example, I once had a functional manager tell me that some team members from another department had a running joke about my habit of recalling email message. She laughed and asked if I knew the email feature didn't work. I did not, but I was taken aback by her crass way of enlightening me. Telling me how foolish I appeared to others was her way of correcting my behavior. She made her point and I am more careful now about recalling emails, but her inept handling of feedback served to change my previously positive view of her.

As a project manager you may not have any direct reports for which you must provide feedback, but if you do, I would advise that you not use this method of messaging.

Negative feedback can also be used to cause divisions between employees. You never want to pit one team member against another by providing praise to one in front of the other, or by meting out discipline publicly. Negative feedback can have lasting effects on the team and can render what little authority you do have ineffectual.

Workplace Etiquette

I bring this up because, believe it or not, some people still have no clue as to what workplace etiquette involves, yet it is an important part of communication. It's simply a list of accepted practices employed when meeting someone for the first time or when attempting to enter an ongoing conversation.

The Welcome Gesture

It's a handshake, a direct gaze and a smile, plain and simple. When you meet someone new, such as a client, sponsor or stakeholder, it is acceptable to extend your hand while displaying a pleasant demeanor. I've been in a lot of meetings lately with younger people who don't bother to introduce themselves, don't extend their hand or even smile at you. They are too busy tapping away on their laptops, texting on their iPhones, or responding to email on their Blackberrys. More seasoned employees are really no better, so a re-examination of this time-honored tradition is worth doing.

A proper welcome shows you have an interest in the other person, that you are open, and that you are courteous. If you have not been practicing this gesture at the start of your meetings, I'd advise you to incorporate it, at least with stakeholders outside your team environment.

The Courteous Interruption

This etiquette technique is sorely lacking in meetings these days. Everyone wants to have their say, and no one will keep quiet long enough for anyone to get a word in edgewise.

Wouldn't it be nice if someone who desired to contribute to a conversation you were having with another person said, "Excuse me, please. May I add this thought?"

Groundbreaking, right?

As your mother, or grandmother, always told you, saying "excuse me" is just common courtesy. Yet, on the job, we have gone so far beyond any semblance of etiquette that it's literally a shame. So why not try using it in your next meeting? I bet the reaction will be shocking, to say the least; it could even break the tension as everyone succumbs to a few giggles. But guess what? If it causes the more heated participants to rethink their attitudes and possibly even their behavior, that's a good thing.

Dress & Grooming

If anything communicates personality, its appearance. Though judging a book by its cover is a human flaw we all possess, it is still used as a character assessment and can mar a person forever. I understand that many technology concerns allow their employees to come to work looking any old way they want, but as a consulting project manager, you should stick to a conventional approach to dressing until you are accepted into the fold. Consultants are not the only ones who need to heed this advice, either. Any image-building workshop will tell you that you are your brand. Your appearance says a lot about you, and once an image is burned into the beholder's mind there is little chance of reversing the impression. Successful brands are evidenced by the results of their image building. Some companies spend millions to mold your view of their products by promoting their good service, attractive packaging and especially name recognition. That's why people were still calling copiers Xerox machines and refrigerators Frigidaires long after these companies lost market share!

Don't think it's just about the style of clothes you wear. Your personal hygiene should also be at acceptable levels. I'd prefer to work with a clean-shaven, bathed, and mouth-washed project manager, as opposed to a scruffy, bad-breathed, musty one. Wouldn't you?

Email, IM and Social Media

Two of the most common communication tools used in the 21st-century office are email and instant messaging (IM). Of course, the wired phone is still valid for conference calls – and occasionally someone may actually stroll into your office to have a face-to-face conversation. Imagine that!

But by and large corporations are joined at the hip with these technological wonders. It's just so much more convenient and faster to share information this way, and it's a proven fact that these tools have greatly increased productivity. As we know from the wildly popular technologies that allow users to connect with others continuously, such as texting, younger workers have come to expect such socialization on the job.

But reliance on these conveniences has its price. One of the disadvantages of email is its impersonal and sometimes dangerous nature. It lends itself to communication without representation or what Daniel Goleman calls "flaming." In a May 18, 2011, interview with Tricycle.com, Goleman explains this activity and why social media in general is making us less empathetic:

> *"Flaming is when somebody's really agitated and they sit down and pound out a message all in caps, and they hit "send" and then immediately regret it; it's a classic online hijack. So, on the downside, there also may be some emotional numbing, some deadening of empathy, and all of that means that we may be fraying social connections as more and more interactions become virtual as on Facebook and less and less face-to-face." (McKeever, 2011)*

If we are on the verge of "fraying our social connections," what will that really mean over the next 20 to 30 years?

I understand where Goleman is coming from. As a user of Facebook, I've noticed that I have 394 friends but only a handful are *really* friends, meaning people I give face time to on a regular basis. This lack of personal contact also lends itself to a lack of personal accountability, and it is becoming an issue for employers who have been forced to discipline FTEs who expound on their work activities in the public forums of the Internet.

As a project manager, you come in contact with a variety of classified or otherwise sensitive information, and you are expected to retain the confidentiality of that information. When managing the different personalities on projects, you may find yourself enforcing company policy as it relates to the use of social media. Granted, it may not be your responsibility to manage to that level; however, if a member of your team is exposed for sharing privileged information or discussing it even in vague generalities, you could be held responsible. The more you know about the company Internet policy and how it will affect the way your team works, the better. Communicating that policy and reiterating it throughout the project lifecycle is a wise practice. Add a column to the communication matrix that lists prohibited mediums, along with an explanation of what is acceptable communication. Taking an early, proactive stance on this matter could prove invaluable later on.

A Word About Buzzwords

Every company has a set of terms, slogans and catchphrases that are commonly used around the office to identify situations, conditions, vendors, customers, etc. They're called *buzzwords*. It's not mandatory for you to know all of them, but understanding what they mean and when to use them can be useful during your tenure at the company, especially if you are a consultant.

Understanding and using the company "lingo" can create a sort of bond between you and those you manage. It shows your interest in the culture and the people and moves you a step closer to acceptance, not only during the project's lifecycle but beyond.

Action Items

- ✔ **Learn the various methods of indirect communication.** Practice recognizing them by asking willing participants to use a few on you as a test. Switch roles and try a few on them, then have them evaluate your effectiveness.

- ✔ **Look the part.** No matter how old the saying gets, it's still true: First impressions are lasting impressions. If you are a project manager, you are likely already putting forth a professional demeanor in your dress and grooming. To an extent, the industry dictates appropriateness, so be aware of what is acceptable at your company or the one where you will be consulting. A shirt and tie for men and a smart business suit for women are always good choices until you are clear on the company requirements. The conclusions drawn based on your appearance will have a lot to do with how others view you on the outside as well as inside.

- ✔ Keep new technology tools **in their proper place**

- ✔ **Know the corporate lingo** and use it appropriately

In addition to these tips, a good read on the nuances of nonverbal communication is any of Daniel Goleman's books on emotional intelligence (EI). Martin Edwards of the U.K. nonprofit trade publication Third Sector describes it this way:

"People with a high level of EI are highly empathetic, they pay people full attention, even when they are very busy themselves and they excel at establishing rapport and building networks. They often show self-deprecating humor and calmly mask their low moods, so that people can never tell if they are having a bad day. They constantly seek subtle, measurable improvements. They are also self-aware and open to change, seeking regular feedback about their performance and paying special attention to negative feedback. Such people get the best out of others, who in turn love working with and for them." (Edwards, 2011)

Managing to Motivate

Real World Advice:
"Be consistent, firm and respectful."
— B.W., Telecommunications

As technology improves and markets become more global the metamorphosis of the business world is inevitable. Whether young or old, subordinate or supervisor, a person's getting and keeping the best job will depend on how savvy he or she is in the area of relationship management.

We briefly touched on the effect that social media is having on our communication styles, causing us to be less interpersonal and more aloof. Unless we find a balance between our gadgets and our face-to-face interactions, this shift could lead to increased misunderstandings.

GenerationTech

Before I start down the road of Generation Xers and Ys, let me say that all generations have an array of work ethics, attitudes and idiosyncrasies, so the following are merely generalizations. Don't take them personally. However, a discussion of personalities would not be complete without mentioning the changing landscape brought on by this new breed of employees that is taking the workplace by storm.

In the past, the world was divided by what was known as a generation gap, so named because of differing cultural tastes that divided teens from their parents. In the 1950s it was rock 'n' roll. In the '60s it was drugs and sex. But today that gap is largely driven by technology. That's why I call the collective group of Xers, Ys and Post-Ys GenerationTech.

There has been a steady, even astounding increase in technological advances since the late 1970s. When the first commercially successful personal computer, the Apple Macintosh, was brought to market in 1977, the first wave of Generation X was being born. The IBM PC first came on the scene in 1981, just ahead of Generation Y.

As a member of the baby boomer generation — which, roughly, includes those born between the mid-1940s and the early 1960s — I recall the early development of digital cell phone technology from when I was a temp at Ericsson. In 1992, most cell phones were huge, clunky things that worked only on analog networks…and few owned them. Now, cell phones define our lives.

No matter which generation you belong to, with technology being so undeniably linked to this younger segment of the workforce, it is worth considering its influence on the job in general and on projects in particular.

Older generations, especially those who are in management, must figure out how to get along with GenTech workers. They must share with and teach these younger co-workers, who bring very different views about work to the office.

If you are a member of GenerationTech, your takeaway from this discussion will be a better understanding of the older generation and the importance it places on values, experience and protocol. After all, until all we boomers are gone, these generations need to work together.

The Generational Divide

To better understand the generation gap as it relates to the workplace, it's important to recap what brought us here.

Back in the day – say from the early 1900s through the 1950s – a job was a symbol of success. This was especially true for men because taking care of a family was a man's first and foremost responsibility. It did not matter so much what kind of work you did; if it was honest work, it was acceptable. If you had a job, people considered you trustworthy. Stores would have no qualms about extending credit to you without a background check. The fact that you worked was a sign of your credit worthiness.

Most men who worked in the manufacturing industries could expect to keep their jobs for at least 30 years. In turn, the company provided generous benefits, including a guaranteed pension at retirement.

So children born in the early part of the Baby Boomer generation — at the end of World War II — had a strong work ethic instilled in them: You work hard and it pays off. There was no middle of the road. These early boomers were generally driven, determined and moral. They believed in playing by the rules and looked down on those who tried to make it the easy way, by cutting corners or cheating the other guy.

The later boomers, born in the mid-'50s to early '60s, grew up during a period of war and civil unrest that was unprecedented. Life was not so cut and dry. Many of these boomers became explorers of all things new and advocates of social change, anxious to make a difference in the world… including the world of work.

For boomers in general, work was not just a means to an end. It was a commitment, a mutual agreement between employer and employee.

Fast forward to 2011 and those boomers are beginning to retire, which means the baton is passing to the first third of GenerationTech: the Gen Xers.

The literature on Generation X has deduced that its members are less likely to remain loyal to a single employer because they want more balance between work and home life (Fontana, 1996). This concept is not foreign to boomers, who early in their careers pushed for reforms, such as paternity leave, parental-care leave and in-home care benefits. So there is some commonality there.

Far from being work-averse, the Gen Xers I know have an admirable work ethic. They just don't want to be tied to their jobs — unless it's via their iPhones. Telecommuting options were created for this generation of employees, mainly because they demanded it. But hey, we boomers are benefiting from that, too!

Now that we see a few things that both boomers and Gen Xers can agree on, why not start there in engaging each other in conversations? These areas of mutual interest can help ease the tension that might be brought on by the age differences. Of course, the actual work has to get done and finding common ground on that score is of paramount importance.

Faced with the loss of knowledge that is beginning to march out the door as boomers retire, Gen X project managers should be planning now for how to get their hands on that information before it's too late. Despite the technological advantage they have on the older crowd, tried-and-true methods instituted by boomers still remain valuable. Experience cannot be taught, but it can be transferred. Find a way to bridge the gap by keeping an open mind, listening and learning. Regardless of whether the old ways make you cringe, work through the irritation. You'll likely find a gem in the mire.

For boomers, no one needs to tell you the impact that having these young, idealistic employees on your team has had on the ability to usher in change. Take advantage of that enthusiasm and resist the urge to be judgmental or, worse, parental. Not everyone fits into the stereotypical mold of his or her generation. If you see traits that need refining, sit your team members down and have a heart to heart. Ask how things are going from their viewpoint and then just listen. Most Gen Xers are ready to take the helm and they want to do things the right way. They need some assistance from you but they also need your confidence in order to know they are going in the right direction. Constructive, open dialog along with some reassuring commendation for a job well done is the first step to penetrating any barriers between you.

I suggest a couple of articles that I have found to be helpful over the years: "A Better Way to Deliver Bad News"

(Manzoni, 2002) and "Teaching Smart People How to Learn" (Argyis, 1991). Both appeared in the *Harvard Business Review*, which, I might add, is an excellent source of help for managers who want to become good leaders.

Moving on to the up-and-coming Gen Y worker, there has been much hyperbole about their impending impact and how they will shatter the world as many of us have come to know it. I was inclined at first to listen to all the exaggeration, but then I read a commentary in *Public Management* magazine that gave me comfort. A Gen Y-er named Gus Caravalho discussed his frustration about job hunting on the Internet, a method he uses almost exclusively. He writes:

"I sometimes wonder, though, whether this method of interaction with organizations...causes all of us applicants to blend into the fog of electronic applications, indistinguishable except for stamps of 'qualified' and 'unqualified.' ...all fields are populated with the same default font, and all applications are printed out in the same format. I worry about this situation not because I am especially fearful of the idea of technology turning me into an anonymous automaton, but rather because I suspect that this lack of personal contact may serve to amplify the ample advantage that "connected" individuals already have towards landing a job..." (Caravalho, 2008)

Whether Caravalho is an exception to all the brouhaha about Gen Y remains to be seen, but his spot-on observation eases my apprehension about his generation and, quite frankly, leads me to believe that they are not all flip and fun-loving; many reflect and agonize, the same as you and I do, over technology concerns.

If those in Generation Y do perform better with structure, as the 'reviews' suggest, that's something already in place at most companies. But those needing constant stimulation and having the flexibility to move in and out of jobs at will could be a challenge to a PM who needs a reliable team for the long haul.

Most of the literature that I've read on this generation indicates that they will single-handedly change the face of employment for decades to come. So, are you ready? How will you, as PM, effectively manage these future team members, stakeholders and possibly even clients?

One thing we do know, as it relates to personalities, is that this new workforce promises to provide a number of challenges to project managers in every industry. Let's review four areas you might take advantage of as a means of addressing these challenges: 1) personal motivators, 2) individualized attention, 3) creative compensation and 4) managed work groups.

While none of these alternatives are necessarily new ideas, they may not have occurred to you as a means of improving morale and lessening the tension on your projects.

Personal Motivators

What motivates one worker may not motivate another. When I was entering the workforce in the early '80s, many of my peer group had two goals in mind: make a name for yourself and, more important, make money.

In 2011, at the writing of this book, the average age of an American was about 37 years. We already know that, in general, Gen Xers seem more interested in balancing job and home life than in money. Understanding how to manage that motivator, while keeping your project on track, may require some creative negotiating on your part.

The subject of personal motivation always make me think of a theory I studied in graduate school called Maslow's Hierarchy of Needs. The premise of this theory is that all humans have a five-tiered set of goals they must meet, ranging from basic needs to enlightenment.

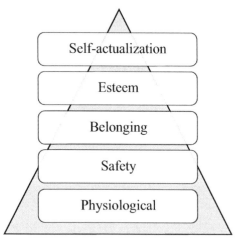

FIGURE 2: MASLOW'S HIERARCHY OF NEEDS

The first level need is physiological (food, shelter, the basics). The second level is safety, such as protection from danger. The third level is the need to belong. This includes love, affection and inclusion. On the fourth level are esteem needs — feeling good about one's self and receiving the indication that others feel good about you, too.

And the top level, which in 1943 Maslow said few of us attain, is the need to achieve our full potential as individuals. He called this self-actualization.

I first studied this hierarchy about six years ago and only recently began to re-evaluate it while researching Generation Y. It appears that the needs of this generation may throw the whole theory out the window! In fact, I'm going to go out on a limb and predict that it will soon look something like the pyramid below: an interconnected set of needs with belonging and esteem being the most important.

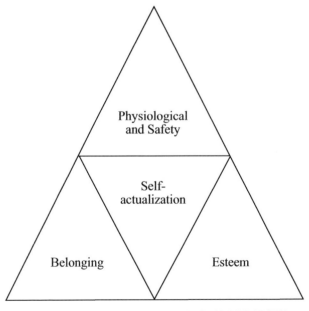

FIGURE 3: REVAMPED VIEW OF MASLOW'S HIERARCHY

I mention these needs because it is important for you as the project manager to investigate what motivates your team members in order to bring out the best in them.

Below are a few suggestions from project managers I surveyed on ways they motivate their teams:

- Ensure clarity and reinforce the goal; do not leave room for ambiguity.
- Allow ownership; some people are motivated by being trusted.
- Reward the whole team for both small and large accomplishments.
- Be a one-on-one manager: know who to push and who to lead.
- Communicate early and often.
- See the individual, not just the role.
- Treat motivation as a project: monitor and control morale during every phase.
- Give the team regular face time and really listen to them.

These suggestions are especially important when your company is hit with major change. For instance, what if IT decides to adopt an all-agile development environment? Or what if downsizing requires retained employees to start doing more with less? Changes like these bring on stress and new pressures that can cause employees to rethink what is really important to them — their job or their sanity.

Individualized Attention

One of the so-called traits of the next generation is the

need to be recognized as unique and special. Therefore, along with proper feedback, project managers should consider assigning work based on the individual strengths and talents each team member brings to the project. Ask yourself what tasks would best utilize each team member's particular talents.

Because change is inherent to projects, you may find it helpful to spend time individually with team members to ascertain how they handle change. Each team member is unique, no matter the generation, so getting a read on his or her change management abilities will help you gauge how difficult it may be for each to make an adjustment.

Creative Compensation

When most employees think of compensation, money is the first thing that comes to mind. But not everyone is motivated by financial incentives. Even some in the baby boomer group have felt the need for alternative types of compensation, such as paternity leave or time off to care for an aged parent.

The idea of compensation for younger generations may require creative thinking on your part. For instance, how can you offer compensation options that apply to the actual work? As project manager, you usually have no control over the paychecks of your team members, but you can compensate them by providing flexibility in their hours, tasks and responsibilities.

If you have team members who are dedicated to your project, coming up with creative compensation options will be much easier than if your team is on loan from a functional manager. However, if you would like to offer ways in which those team members can benefit from a creative compensation idea, why not schedule some time with that manager to see if the two of you might be able to make it work?

One creative compensation method that seems to have had success with project teams is flextime, which contrasts with the usual nine-to-five workday. One way that flextime can be segmented is by allowing two team members to do what is known as *job sharing*. For example, a morning developer performs certain tasks, while others are assigned to an afternoon developer. Each employee would work four hours per day, essentially sharing a job. (If that is what they both prefer, be sure you are authorized to allow part-time workers.)

Another option is the *split shift*, which allows an employee to come in for a few hours, then leave for a few, and come back for the remainder of the day. This option is not recommended for projects utilizing an agile methodology; however, it can work for other types of environments and is a great way to give employees a "breather" if their work is particularly stressful.

A third alternative is *flexible hours*. Let's say you have an employee who commutes an hour or more each day. Why not allow that person to work an afternoon shift, or possibly arrive or leave later?

As one of our surveyed PMs suggested, consider adopting group incentives that allow workers to benefit as a team, such as allowing the team to plan an offsite gathering. Or give them the option to alter the weekly status meeting with an awards presentations or catered lunches from their favorite restaurant.

At a web firm where I worked, we created an award — a frog (don't ask) — that moved among team members. If you did something great one week, you were privileged to keep the frog at your desk for everyone to see. We were also rewarded with special treats: one month that we made our numbers, the company gave us free drinks and snacks for a week. The point is to keep it interesting, lively and fun. These kinds of activities can assist in keeping the team engaged and cooperative.

Managed Groups

A lot of research has been done on self-directed teams, but in many cases the experiment has not proven to be the success most companies expected. The direction that needs to be taken, in my opinion, is to allow groups to exist within a more structured framework, what I called *managed groups*. As the title implies, these teams should have oversight and a clear set of guidelines at the beginning. In time, as they show their ability to manage autonomously, the baseline can be built upon with additional, more independent processes. This is a departure from traditional self-directed teams, and for good reason — it takes the fear out of the process for upper management by easing into the team concept. It also lessens the uncertainty of direction for workers, both young and old.

The managed group approach is heralded by a number of

researchers who have studied the use of self-directed teams. Their general consensus is that, without the proper amount of structure, monitoring and guidance, workers can become unproductive, fall into a group-think mentality, and actually become less effective than they were prior to forming the group. The article, "Teamwork Takes Work" (Norman & Zawacki, 1991), explains how these groups can have added benefits by teaching members skills that go beyond the normal work tasks. Self-directed teams are usually expected to handle their own scheduling, training and member appraisals. These additional responsibilities, they say, can have a positive effect on self-worth as well as on job satisfaction.

The Gender Gap

Personal needs differ not only from generation to generation and person to person, but also between the sexes. So I consider gender worth noting here.

It's no secret that women and men are inherently different in the way they attack work tasks. During the gender gap of the 1980s, women aspired to run things and so were motivated by promotions and gaining increasing responsibilities within the organization. Unfortunately, we hit what was called the "glass ceiling," which illustrated the limits on women who desired reaching executive status.

Nowadays, there are more women in the workforce than men, and many of them are running things. According to the *Global Gender Gap Report 2010* (Hausmann, Tyson, & Zahidi, 2010), North America has closed 70 percent of the gender gap in the areas of health, education and economics.

But keep in mind that there is still much work to be done to level the playing field for women. If you are a man managing women on your team, drawing them out to discover what motivates them can be tricky. Be careful not to patronize them nor treat them with kid gloves.

To lessen any confusion on how to make your approach, conduct regular touch points with your female team members. These should include questions that allow them to expound on their workday and to share issues without fear of reprisal or condescension. Above all, women need to feel they are in an atmosphere of fairness. As the old saying goes, "what's good for the goose is good for the gander." The women on your team are not your wives, your daughters or your sisters. Treat them with the same respect and trust you would give your male team members. If you do, the payoff can be huge.

Action Items

✔ No matter which generation you hail from, maintain an attitude of inclusion and a willingness to cooperate and understand.

✔ Find ways to seek common ground between your generational attitudes and those of your team members, sponsor or other stakeholders.

✔ Be aware of the motivations and needs of all your team members, male and female.

✔ Try new ways to motivate your team. Work with Human Resources, if applicable.

✔ Read Daniel Goleman's *Emotional Intelligence in the Workplace*.

Putting It All into Perspective

Real World Advice:
"Realize that some conflicts are inevitable.
Resolve them quickly, or they will only get worse."
— D.E., Information Technology

If you are a new project manager, the information in this book may seem overwhelming and you may not know where to start. That's normal. Keep in mind that no matter how many years of experience a PM possesses, there is always something new to learn when managing people.

That's where leadership comes in. Up until now, we've considered a myriad of circumstances that could occur, along with options for mitigating them. But we have not discussed leadership styles, the approaches that can make or break any situation. Before we wrap things up, let's review what Daniel Goleman calls the Six Leadership Styles. Determining which ones you use now, and which you should begin using, will be a big help in making your project relationships run smoothly.

In the research article "Leadership That Gets Results," Goleman lists the following types:

- **Coercive** — demands immediate compliance
- **Authoritative** — mobilizes people toward a vision
- **Affiliative** — creates harmony, builds emotional bonds
- **Democratic** — forges consensus
- **Pacesetting** — sets high performance standards
- **Coaching** — develops future leaders

Of these types, Goleman says "only four of the six consistently have a positive effect on climate and results." Can you guess which four?

As my mother used to say, you can catch more flies with honey than with vinegar. Because no one likes to be bullied, we know the *coercive* style is not in the group. But which other style is ineffective? If you guessed *authoritative* you're wrong. The answer is *pacesetting*.

A pacesetter leads by example. In fact, he expects his example to be followed — *to the letter*. His exacting demands may start out with positive intent, but the unreasonable expectations can backfire and cause team members to feel micro-managed and distrusted. Goleman suggests that a leader who uses this style should attempt to balance it by being more *affiliative*; developing empathy for others and improving communication skills.

The style found to be best suited for success was the *authoritative*, which ranked highest in the areas of flexibility, responsibility, standards, rewards, clarity and commitment

—items considered drivers of the modern-day work environment. (Goleman, March-April 2000)

The results of this research is worth reviewing in full, so I highly recommend you read this article.

To conclude, let's recap the major areas outlined in previous chapters so you can keep them in mind:

1. Get to know the personalities on your project, either by a formal assessment, team-building activities or one-on-one interviews. Do this early on and follow up regularly. Assign tasks that fit your team members' personalities.
2. Find out how things are done at the company from those in a position to know, then build your information store so that you can call upon it at the proper time.
3. Understand the effect of company culture on your team members and stakeholders. Don't brush it off as unimportant, but rather learn as much as you can about it and keep it in mind as you guide your team.
4. Identify your adversaries and devise a plan to disarm them before they disrupt your project.
5. Communicate, communicate and communicate. Do so to the right people at the right time, using the right medium and the right approach.
6. Recognize and understand the nuances of indirect messaging. Learn to make it work for you.
7. Do not discount the new generational thinking coming into the workforce; instead, nurture and guide it. Do not ignore

the wisdom offered by seasoned employees who may not only be older, but also wiser. Use their experience to your advantage.
8. Beware of office politics and all that entails. Be ready to manage it effectively while avoiding any appearance of contributing to it.
9. Check your leadership style and make sure it's working for you.

One of the best expressions of self-management I've ever heard, and what I consider the perfect summation to this book, comes from Rudyard Kipling's poem "If." Enjoy it — and remember, projects ARE PEOPLE, TOO!

> If you can keep your head when all about you
> Are losing theirs and blaming it on you;
> If you can trust yourself when all men doubt you,
> But make allowance for their doubting too;
>
> If you can wait and not be tired by waiting,
> Or being lied about, don't deal in lies,
> Or being hated, don't give way to hating,
> And yet don't look too good, nor talk too wise;
>
> If you can dream — and not make dreams your master;
> If you can think — and not make thoughts your aim,
> If you can meet with Triumph and Disaster
> And treat those two impostors just the same;

If you can bear to hear the truth you've spoken
Twisted by knaves to make a trap for fools,
Or watch the things you gave your life to, broken,
And stoop and build 'em up with worn out tools;

If you can make one heap of all your winnings
And risk it on one turn of pitch-and-toss,
And lose, and start again at your beginnings
And never breathe a word about your loss;

If you can force your heart and nerve and sinew
To serve your turn long after they are gone,
And so hold on when there is nothing in you
Except the Will which says to them: 'Hold on!'

If you can talk with crowds and keep your virtue,
Or walk with kings — nor lose the common touch,
If neither foes nor loving friends can hurt you,
If all men count with you, but none too much;

If you can fill the unforgiving minute
With sixty seconds' worth of distance run,
Yours is the Earth and everything that's in it,
And — which is more — you'll be a Man, my son!

BIBLIOGRAPHY

Argyis, C. (1991). *Teaching Smart People How to Learn.* Harvard Business Review, 5-16.

Birkman. (n.d.). *Birkman.* Retrieved from Birkman - Reaching Further: http://www.birkman.com.

Caravalho, G. (2008, June). *On Hiring Generation Y.* Public Management (PM). Reprinted with permission. Published and copyrighted by ICMA (International County/City Management Association), Washington, D.C., Public Management: ICMA.org/PM.

Edwards, M. (2011, June 6). *Emotional intelligence is key to being a good leader.* Reprinted with permission from Third Sector: http://thirdsector.co.uk.

EEOC. (n.d.). *Equal Employment Opportunity Commission, Sexual Harassment.* Retrieved from EEOC: http://archive.eeoc.gov/types/sexual_harassment.html.

Fontana, D. (1996, February 12). *Getting to Know Genera-*

tion X is Half the Battle for Managers. American Banker, pp. Vol. 161, Issue 28, page 10.

Goleman, Daniel (March-April 2000). *Leadership that gets results*. Harvard Business Review.

Hausmann, Tyson, & Zahidi. (2010). *Global Gender Gap Report 2010*. Retrieved from World Economic Forum: http://www.weforum.org/women-leaders-and-gender-parity.

Kegan, R., & Laskow Lahey, L. (2001, November). *The Real Reason People Won't Change*. Harvard Business Review, pp. 85-92.

Littman, J., & Hershon, M. (2009). I Hate People! quiz. In *I Hate People! Kick Loose from the Overbearing and Underhanded Jerks at Work and Get What You Want Out of Your Job*. New York: Reprinted with permission by Little, Brown. Available on amazon.com.

Manzoni, J. F. (2002, September). *A Better Way to Deliver Bad News*. Harvard Business Review, pp. 2-7.

McKeever, M. (2011, May 18). *The Brain and Emotional Intelligence: An Interview with Daniel Goleman*. Reprinted with permission from Tricycle: Awake in the World: tricycle.com.

Mind Tools. (n.d.). *How Are Your Communication Skills?* Reprinted with permission from Mind Tools© Ltd, All rights reserved: http://www.mindtools.com/pages/article/newCS_99.htm.

Myers-Briggs. (n.d.). My MBTI *Personality Type*. Retrieved from Myersbriggs.org: http://www.myersbriggs.org/my-mbti-personality-type/mbti-basics.

Norman, C., & Zawacki, R. (1991, April 1). *Teamwork Takes Work*. Computerworld , pp. 77-78.

Spiegel, A. (2011, July 6). *To Prevent False IDs, Police Lineups Get Revamped*. Retrieved from and reprinted with permission. National Public Radio: npr.org.

Spragins, B. (2007). *Large Project Partnering: T-REX Projects' Success a Model for the Industry*. FMI Quarterly, pp. 25-35.

Thoms, P., Moore, K., & Scott, K. (1996). *The Relationship between self-efficacy for participating in managed work groups and the big five personality dimensions*. Journal of Organizational Behavior, vol. 17, pp, 349-362.

TABLE OF FIGURES

FIGURE 1:
  COMMUNICATION MODEL   80
FIGURE 2:
  MASLOW'S HIERARCHY OF NEEDS   114
FIGURE 3:
  REVAMPED VIEW OF MASLOW'S HIERARCHY   115

ABOUT THE AUTHOR

FAITH KNIGHT is a project manager, journalist and author. Knight's passion for writing began long before her first story was inked while a stringer for the Dayton Daily News. From print, she went on to a television news career that lasted nearly 15 years, along the way she would move to the web and the staffs of NBC Washington, MSNBC and Discovery Channel. When she decided to leave the news business, her unique skills led her to the field of project management and a variety of new roles and employers.

Her interest in personality management began when she was hired into her first job at an automotive parts manufacturing plant. As she observed the relationship between employees and supervisors, she noticed an unwritten edict of communication and protocol, not only between worker and employer but also between employees, and between supervisors. These subtleties both fascinated and concerned her.

The number of strange rules and customs seemed to increase as she moved from the blue-collar industry into the corporate world, with more serious consequences in the latter. Office politics, such as quid pro quo, took place during the course of the workday and often determined the fate of a person's livelihood and even ruined careers.

But the effects of The Game took on new meaning when she became a project manager and was able to see how, if left unchecked or unmanaged, this "sport" could wreak havoc on months and even years of hard work.

It was with a desire to arm others with this knowledge that led her to write *Projects Are People, Too*.

Made in the USA
Charleston, SC
18 December 2011